A Time To Remember

A Tale of the Viet Nam Conflict

by

Cecil Barr Currey

authorHOUSE

1663 LIBERTY DRIVE, SUITE 200
BLOOMINGTON, INDIANA 47403
(800) 839-8640
www.authorhouse.com

© 2004 Cecil Barr Currey.
All Rights Reserved.

No part of this book may be reproduced, stored in a retrieval system, or transmitted by any means without the written permission of the author.

First published by AuthorHouse 05/14/04

ISBN: 1-4184-5840-6 (e)
ISBN: 1-4184-3519-8 (sc)
ISBN: 1-4184-3518-X (dj)

Library of Congress Control Number: 2004092844

Printed in the United States of America
Bloomington, Indiana

This book is printed on acid-free paper.

On *Innocence Dies* (1992):

"Cecil Currey, has captured both the sense and the senses of Viet Nam with his descriptions, revealing its sights, sounds and smell. His technical understanding of the people, the places, and the army at war grounds this material in reality, taking it out of the realm of fiction, thus making it much more of a historical novel. Characters and places seem real. The sadness and sorrow of war and all its gore is vividly described with intensity and insight. The egos of warriors and would-be/ wanna-be heroes is aptly reported. Currey shows that the self-interests of high ranking officers sometimes supercedes the safety and security of their own soldiers. This is a satisfying work. The book is a keeper."--Chaplain (Brigadier General) Wayne W. Hoffman, AUS (Ret.), former Assistant Chief of Chaplains for Reserve Affairs who had thirty-eight years of service, active, reserve, and National Guard.

On *A Time to Remember:*

". . . The author of *Innocence Dies* shows once again in this new book that he is not only a seasoned writer, but a painter of pictures as well, one who offers shadows of reality as an art. . . . This is a well-crafted and thoughtful account of people enduring great burdens. . . . The plot line, character development, movement of scene, and realism of content flow together marvelously. . . .A mood prevails throughout this story that there may be more factual content here than expected. In Currey's book there are painful questions about warfare, humanity, and integrity that the Army has never resolved."

–Major Donald W. Hamilton, USAR, author of *The Art of Insurgency* (Greenwood Publishing Group, 1998).

"This is an absolutely authentic depiction of the Vietnam experience. I felt like I was there again, suffering, wrestling with issues of right and wrong. From beginning to end I was spellbound by this book. As I got close to the last page, I dreaded it being over."

–Chaplain (Colonel) Jerry Autry, USA (Ret.), Vietnam vet and holder of the Silver Star for his actions in combat and the Purple Heart.

This book is dedicated to the officers and men who were captured by the enemy in Viet Nam and to one man who managed to escape, Nick Rowe. Lieutenant Rowe was captured in the Mekong Delta in 1963. For five years, Rowe was held prisoner by the Viet Cong, suffering daily mental and physical torture. Yet he never gave up, never signed a "confession," and finally, sick and weak, he found opportunity to make the only escape on record by an American officer from a Viet Cong prison. Following his escape he was promoted to captain and then major. He later wrote *Five Years to Freedom*, one of the best books on survival ever published. He returned to the Army, to Special Forces, in March 1981 as a lieutenant colonel to head the Green Beret survival training program.

"A true war story is never moral. It does not instruct, nor encourage virtue, nor suggest models of proper human behavior, nor restrain men from doing the things men have always done. If a story seems moral, do not believe it. If at the end of a war story you feel uplifted, or if you feel that some small bit of rectitude has been salvaged from the larger waste, then you have been made the victim of a very old and terrible lie. There is no rectitude whatsoever. There is no virtue. As a first rule of thumb, therefore, you can tell a true war story by its absolute and uncompromising allegiance to obscenity and evil."–from Tim O'Brien, *The Things they Carried.*

* * * * *

Dulce et Decorum Est

Bent double, like old beggars under sacks,
Knock-kneed, coughing like hags, we cursed through sludge,
Till on the haunting flares we turned our backs
And towards our distant rest began to trudge.
Men marched asleep. Many had lost their boots
But limped on, blood-shod. All went lame; all blind,
Drunk with fatigue, deaf even to the hoots
Of tired, outstripped Five-Nines that dropped behind.

Gas! Gas! Quick, boys!–An ecstasy of fumbling,
Fitting the clumsy helmets just in time;
But someone still was yelling out and stumbling,
And flound'ring like a man in fire or lime . . . .
Dim, through the misty panes and thick green light,
As under a green sea, I saw him drowning.
In all my dreams, before my helpless sight,
He plunges at me, guttering, choking, drowning.

If in some smothering dreams you too could pace
Behind the wagon that we flung him in,

And watch the white eyes writing in his face,
His hanging face, like a devil's sick of sin,
If you could hear, at every jolt, the blood
Come gargling from the froth-corrupted lungs,
Obscene as cancer, bitter as the cud
Of vile, incurable sores on innocent tongues,
My friend, you would not tell with such high zest
To children ardent for some desperate glory,
The old Lie, *Dulce et Decorum est*
Pro Patria mori.

−Written by Wilfred Owen, killed on the Western Front during the Great War on 4 November 1918, aged 25, dead just seven days before the Armistice that ended the conflict.

Professional Writings

Quaker Pacifism in Kansas, 1833-1945

Benjamin Franklin and the Radicals, 1765-1775

Road to Revolution: Benjamin Franklin in England

Code Number 72: Ben Franklin, Patriot or Spy?

The Craft and Crafting of History

Reason and Revelation: The Natural Theology of John Duns Scotus

Guide to Images of America: A Text

Self-Destruction: The Disintegration and Decay of the U.S. Army During the Viet Nam Conflict

Follow Me and Die: The Destruction of an American Army Division During the Second World War

With Wings as Eagles: The History of Army Flight from a Branch of Aviation to Aviation Branch

Edward Lansdale: The Unquiet American

For God and Country: The Story of a Constutional Challenge to the Army Chaplaincy

Victory at any Cost: The Genius of Viet Nam's Senior General Vo Nguyen Giap

Long Binh Jail: An Oral History of the U.S. Army's Notorious Prison in Viet Nam

Genealogical Studies

A Currey Family History

Memories and Reminiscences: An Early Life

Memories and Reminiscences: The Middle Years

Memories and Reminiscences: Culmination

Children's Fiction

Mara and the Manatee of God

McKenna's Book

Adult Fiction

Innocence Dies: A Viet Nam War Novel

A Time to Remember: A Tale of the Viet Nam Conflict

ACKNOWLEDGMENTS

The author wishes to make special mention of the help given to him by the following people:

Mr. Donald Sampson, LLB., Central City, Nebraska, who gave invaluable advice about the court-martial and who kept me straight on legal matters. I hope I have also adequately addressed his other concerns.

Mr. Stephen D'Angelo, R.N., Tampa, Florida, director of cardiac rehabilitation at University Community Hospital, without whom I could not have divined the necessary medical procedures used in the rehabilitation of Douglas MacArthur Andrews and Jan Lech Szigmond. He also wanted more details about the trip south hazarded by Andrews and Szigmond. Stephen, I hope you like the expanded material.

Mrs. Jackie Sampson of Central City, Nebraska who kept me faithful not only to my old home town but who asked pointed questions and who found many typographical errors I would not otherwise have seen.

Mrs. Maria Richards, of Wesley Chapel, Florida whose careful and insightful reading of an early version of this manuscript was of real value. Her interest and willingness to help are appreciated.

Mrs. Maxine (Sapp) Romohr, Gresham, Nebraska, once my journalism instructor in high school and who fifty years later is still my friend. The care with which she read this manuscript is exceeded only by her kindness and concern for others. She is one of the few truly good people I have known.

Mr. Ernest Hubbard, who conscientiously reads my stories, and whose reactions I treasure.

And, of course, I thank Laura Gene (Hewett) Currey, who has been my wife lo these many years and who does her best always to help and encourage me in my endeavors.

AUTHOR'S NOTE:

A Time to Remember has not been an easy book to write. It may also not be an easy book for some to read. In its prequel, *Innocence Dies*, I tried to write an exciting story that would be militarily correct about combat and small unit leadership, about Viet Nam and its people, about the mistakes made there by our civilian and military leaders, and about how extended action in combat can erode one's mental and moral equilibrium. Reactions from hundreds of readers–military and civilian--indicated that I succeeded in creating such a tale.

For nearly three decades I have been studying how American prisoners of war were treated in Viet Nam by the Viet Cong guerrilla fighters of the South and the North Vietnamese. I have long wanted to write of this canker on the face of civilization to help fill an existing void. Although some former prisoners have told of their experiences while in enemy hands, little of a popular nature has been written on this subject.

In many cases they were treated worse than beasts, in inhuman ways by men who in other times and other places have been the kindest and most courteous of all the people with whom I have lived and worked. Some prisoners were driven to the brink of sanity and even beyond. Many died from mistreatment. Some have never been accounted for. All were scarred in their minds and souls by the years they spent in the hands of the enemy. *A Time to Remember* tells their story. The pages that tell of torture will seem to some to be too extended. Let all readers know this and beware.

Every form of torture described in this book was really applied to our POWs, to some more than others, but the threat of such hung heavily over the heads of all. As you read herein of life in a northern prison think of the one named *Hoa Lo* or in Vietnamese "the oven," called by Americans the 'Ha Noi Hilton' where many of our POWs were held, where many were subjected to the most horrific of tortures and where some died from mistreatment. Although I describe many of the ways of torture herein used on those POWs, know that there were others used–even more horrible ones-- that I have chosen to omit from my story.

As you read of the 'tap code,' know that it was really used by our soldiers and airmen to communicate with one another in an environment where speech and human contact was often forbidden them and closely supervised when it was allowed.

The pages that tell of the escape from prison and the long trek southward to the 17th parallel and to American lines are based on real experiences. One man, just one, managed to accomplish that near miraculous feat and I wanted to honor his courage and dedication.

The little men of the mountains are there today as they have been for a millennium. They still maintain their own cultural ways and continue to bear resentment against the lowland Vietnamese.

The paragraphs that describe spousal abuse are also based on reality. I have known women who have suffered every one of the torments described in this book. Again, some may say less detail would have sufficed. Perhaps. But the terrible pain and desolation such women feel would not have been fully described in fewer pages.

The characters of Douglas MacArthur Andrews, Donald Stoddard, Jan Lech Szigmond, Paul Eastley, Vernon Moore and others are all composites but not mirror images of men I have known and worked with during my thirty-nine years and five months in uniform, serving both as an enlisted man and, later, as a Reserve officer.

As in *Innocence Dies*, the little Nebraska town of Central City plays a large role in this story. There really is such a town and it is much like I have portrayed it in both novels.

Thus in many ways, although fictional, this is a true story.

CHAPTER ONE

"Am I my brother's keeper?"–Genesis IV: 10b

He slowly returned to consciousness, consumed by the pain in his chest. It was more than he could bear and once again he passed out, wondering all the while what it was that was jolting him, making the pain even worse.

* * * * *

Again he awoke, feeling the agony that sat on his chest. He reached for its center only to be swept with the scourges of agony. In the short time he was able to touch his chest, he felt a stickiness and, looking at his fingers, saw that they were covered with blood. The jolting was still there and, painfully turning his head, he discovered that he was lying in the back of a beat-up old pickup that bounced along a nearly nonexistent road. He noticed that his face was stiff with dried blood and tried to recall why that should be. Why the blood? Why the pain in his chest? He faded once again into nothingness.

* * * * *

Images flashed through his mind, painful, aching, scourging, tormenting. Flickering visions of death and life. He thought of soldiers he had known: Weathers. Pappas. Hays and Arnold. Cooper. Samuels. Gomez. Jimmy van Buren and Pete Dobbs. Of Gaunilow writhing in pain from burns only finally to die in agony later at Brooke Army Medical Center in San Antonio. Carl Palmer. Hughes. Lee. Gonzalo Gonzalez. Harry Kinback's blood dripping from a tree. Smith and Muldoon. Hugh Early. Frank Doomes. Nelson and Tully. Larry Tremens' blinded eyes and Oliver Ensenlaube's blasted knee. The wretched and pitiful Rafael Jesus Terife de Palenque. Aaron "Red Man" Finch. Leroy Johnson. George Catlett. Staff Sergeant Dave Hensley. Bill Post. Hugh Doty. Jules Carroll and Paolo Bertinelli. First Sergeant Harold Spruance. Cynical Colonel Vernon "Savage" Moore. His battalion commander Jeremiah Barrett. His dear friend Don Stoddard. He saw the faces of others whose names he could no longer recall. He thought of his friend Sergeant First Class Jan Szigmond, deserted by his comrades at the bunker and left to die there. So many of those faces were now dead and he could not remember why. He groaned with the pain of those memories.

* * * * *

He opened his eyes. This time he noticed an Asian man sitting near him in the bed of the pickup, staring at him with dark impenetrable eyes. The unsmiling man wiped his forehead with a damp cloth and it came away bloody. Suddenly he knew who and where he was. His name was Douglas MacArthur Andrews, always known as Doug. He was a soldier–a captain–in the United States Army. And he was somewhere in Viet Nam in the midst of an undeclared war. The pain in his chest was as if some small rodent sat there, gnawing its way to his heart. His lids grew heavy and closed once again.

* * * * *

He thought of his fiancé, Army nurse Nancy West, and the hope they shared for a future life together. He thought of his family and his home in Nebraska and of how he had once been so certain about the differences between right and wrong. Suddenly he remembered the face of his battalion's *chieu hoi*, Le Qui Thanh, and he recalled lying beside a dead man whose blood he had smeared on his face and how, looking up, he saw Thanh glaring at him. Thanh pointed a rifle. Flame burst from the barrel and pain blossomed in his chest. Oh my god. Oh my god. Over and again the words ran through his mind.

* * * * *

Now his memory was filling out. He had been assigned to Viet Nam. Starting as a second lieutenant platoon leader, he had come at last to command a company. He had been sent to a field hospital to recover from malaria, intestinal parasites and skin covered with jungle rot. He saw again the face of Nancy West, dressed in her uniform standing beside his bed, caring for him. Then the two of them were in Hawaii on leave, exploring one another and Honolulu. He loved her. He wanted to go home, back to Nebraska, back to Central City, to be with his mother and father and beloved sister, Laura. He wanted his parents to know Nancy and to come to love her as a daughter.

He was so close to accomplishing that. Only a few days remained before his DEROS date when the Freedom Bird would take him from this pesthole back to civilization and home. The wheels of the truck dropped into a pothole and clawed their way back out. Doug fainted from the pain that pursued him.

* * * * *

The motion had stopped. He could no longer feel the metal truck bed beneath him. Now he lay within a rude hut on a thin pallet atop a low table. The floor was earthen, the walls of bamboo, the roof made from palm fronds. Although still agonizing, somehow the pain in his chest had lessened while he was unconscious. Doug felt hands touching him and looked around. Beside him was a diminutive man holding a medical probe. The man spoke to him in Vietnamese, of which Doug understood not a word. Two other men entered the hut and positioned themselves near him, one holding down his arms while the other clung to his feet. The first man spoke again, and then pressed the tip of the probe into the wound on Doug's chest. It slid inward as Doug bucked and reared and screamed in pain. Darkness fell upon him.

* * * * *

He was outside Yen Song (3), conducting a sweep of the area searching for the Viet Cong 48th Local Force Battalion. Moments earlier, Lieutenant Norman Crosse had triggered a booby trap that left his body broken while blood poured from broken vessels. He died within seconds. Then from within the village someone had fired a rifle at Doug's platoon. Staff Sergeant Leroy Johnson's body sagged to the ground, blood seeping through the fingers clutched to his face. Skip Condon looked frantically at the dead officer and back at Johnson's body. Doug recalled running to the scene and crouching beside the bodies, his M-79 at the ready. What was left of Crosse's body continued to twitch.

"What happened, Condon?" he asked.

"Sir. We don't know. Everything was smooth. Then all of a sudden the Lieutenant blew up. Then someone in the ville shot Johnson." There was another sharp crack from the settlement and a bullet ploughed into the earth nearby. Bill Post lay a few yards away, his face wet with tears. Leroy had been his friend. They had bunked and eaten and humped together for the better part of a year. Now Johnson lay dead in the dust with a shattered head. Post's anger grew.

Sergeant First Class Harold Spruance lay trembling. He seemed outside his own body, detached, observant, watching himself quiver. Only two friends in all Viet Nam and now one of them lay dead, killed by some sniper. Stretched beside him, Captain Andrews shook his head, tears of anger and loss burning his eyes. Something would have to be done. Those responsible must be punished. It was impossible for him to endure this stoically. His soul cried out for vengeance.

* * * * *

Doug came awake slowly. Experimentally he touched his aching chest only to discover that it was covered with bandages. The tiny physician stood beside his pallet, his face wreathed in smiles. *"Ciao Ong,"* he said and held up a metal washbasin in which rattled a steel jacketed rifle bullet. He nodded his head. "You . . . be . . . o.k.," he said with some difficulty. Doug weakly returned his smile. Maybe he would live after all. Maybe, if he was lucky, he might one day again hold Nancy West in his arms. Maybe, in some still dawn hour, when his father Chalmers, unable to sleep, had risen early to sit alone in the dining alcove drinking a cup of coffee, maybe, just maybe, he might also sit with him and talk of things past and future.

Doug looked around the hut. Previously he had thought he was the only inhabitant. Now he saw other tables, clothed with thin pallets, on which lay men who, he calculated, were aged from about sixteen to forty. He was sure he had been taken to a Viet Cong field hospital. His suspicions were confirmed when Le Qui Thanh came through the door. Doug winced. This was the man who shot him. What was he planning now?

Thanh came to his bedside, his dark eyes glittering with hatred. He stood for a moment absorbing the scene. Then he spoke. *"Dai uy,* I was once your second battalion's *chieu hoi.* Doug understood *Dai uy.* It was the Vietnamese phrase for "captain." He also understood

4

all too well the phrase *chieu hoi*. The term referred to a person who had fought with the Viet Cong and who, often sick or wounded and despairing, was promised fair treatment, good food, and medical care if he came into Republic of Viet Nam or American lines and surrendered. Many thereafter became translators or scouts or performed some other such purpose for the American troops. Others simply faded back into the jungle after their recuperation. Cynics called the program a Viet Cong opportunity for R & R–rest and recuperation.

Thanh continued, his voice filled with anger. "You destroyed my village of Kinh Duc. I had to kill some of my own relatives there to keep them from revealing to you that I was Viet Cong. Now it is destroyed, home only to beasts of the jungle. At Muc Dien, your artillery killed my betrothed–my Nguyen Thi Thu Thuy. It blew her body apart. There was hardly even anything left to bury. You have taken everything from me. Now I have only my hatred. You now stand accused as the butcher of the village of Yen Song (3). I am glad I did not kill you, *Dai uy*. You deserve to live so you can be forced to die over and over again." With those words, Thanh leaned over Doug and spat full in his face. Then he turned on his heel and left the hut. Doug never saw him again. In due time, weak and distraught, Andrews closed his eyes and slept.

* * * * *

Doug felt a calmness beyond anger or rage or reason. Somehow it had to end. Two more of his friends lay dead beside him. No more. He pushed a white phosphorus round into the magazine of his M-79, walked toward the ville and when he came within range he aimed at the nearest thatched hut. It exploded into flames, the Willie Peter white hot in its destructive fury.

"How do you like that?" he shrieked. "I'll make you bastards pay for this." He strode further into the village of Yen Song (3). Behind him came Bill Post, sixteen in one hand, magazines in the other, taped end to end, so that with a flip of his hand they could be reversed when one ran empty. Post rammed the magazine home, tapped it on the end and switched his sixteen to automatic fire.

5

Paolo Bertinelli, his radio set forgotten, reached into the pouch on his cartridge belt and pulled two hand grenades from it as he ran after the others. Tears wet his face. In that moment all his training deserted him. No RTO was ever to leave his radio behind. But Paolo did, without thought.

* * * * *

Doug awoke with a start, his body sweaty. Infection from the septic conditions in the hut coursed through his blood. His face was hot, flushed, his temperature hovering about 104 degrees. He called out. No one came to succor him. The only result was a flurry of angry Vietnamese curses from the other wounded men in the hut. The tiny physician momentarily looked inside the room. He had no medicines, not even rubber gloves. He had no tubs in which to boil water to sterilize his instruments. He had operated on Doug to cleanse the channel made by the bullet's course through his chest with instruments that had never seen an autoclave. The Viet Cong supply system was supposed to be sending him several bottles of antiseptic. Perhaps that might help men like the *Dai uy*, if it ever arrived. Shipments were unpredictable. He shrugged. There was nothing he could do for this foreign soldier who would either live or die on his own.

* * * * *

His face suffused with anger, Skip Condon stood waving the men of his squad toward him. Soldiers from first squad came along also. Bill Post was now far ahead, moving into the hamlet firing his sixteen. Jules Carroll, Hugh Doty, John Anderson and others from first squad fell into place behind Condon.

Staff Sergeant Dave Hensley, second squad leader, shouted at his men. "Remember what they taught us. It's an enemy ville if even one hostile round is fired at us. So wipe it out. Shoot the bastards!" He pointed his sixteen at a water buffalo and hosed it with a full magazine of bullets. The animal collapsed bellowing, in a bloody heap. "Shoot the goddam cows."

A third bullet fired from the hamlet caught George Catlett in the chest, throwing him backward off his feet. He coughed and died. Shores and Gurtleff, beside him, stared down at their fallen friend,

6

then cursed and fired at the few fleeing people they could see among the huts before them.

Rick Carney slipped the pin of a fragmentation grenade and arced it through the air as far into the settlement as he could throw it. Ben Jackson and Edgar Franklin, second squad's M-60 team, pushed the weapon's bipod legs into place and fired into nearby hooches.

This was no longer Captain Douglas MacArthur Andrew's disciplined, trained, and cohesive strike force that moved into the ville and toward the few frightened inhabitants who had not had time to flee. They still milled in confusion as they watched the men of Doug's command walking toward them. Those men were a mob seeking blood.

* * * * *

Pain gnawed at his consciousness. Doug opened his eyes. The hooch now had an antiseptic smell. The pain from his chest was caused by a diminutive Vietnamese woman, probably a Viet Cong nurse, who was swabbing his wound with iodine. It burned into the raw tissues of his chest. Doug screamed. The woman patted his arm and with a damp cloth wiped his face. She smiled at him. When he was able to do so, Doug looked around. The physician seemed to be gone for good, leaving this woman in charge. Light streamed in through the openings in the walls–they were hardly real windows. He saw several large cockroaches running across the counter where the nurse had placed her meager supplies. Geckos played in the palm fronds of the ceiling.

"Better. More better," the woman said. "Soon sit. Walk."

* * * * *

Time faded in and out for Doug. The nurse tended to him, changing his dressings, feeding him, bathing him, helping him with his sanitary needs. He soon tired of the rice fed him with every meal and of the soup she called *Pho*. He became ever more adept at eating with chopsticks. He set a goal for himself. He would practice until he was able to use them to pick up the last grains of rice from his bowl, scattered singly within it.

7

The days passed in quiet succession, each much like the one before and promising to be like the one to follow. Slowly Doug grew stronger. He sat up. Then, with the nurse to steady him, he put a tentative foot on the floor and forced himself to take a few steps.

One afternoon the little physician reappeared. With him was an interpreter whose rudimentary English enabled Doug and the doctor to speak with one another. The man told Doug that for a time he doubted the *Dai uy* would live. The bullet had done much damage. He had done more harm to the damaged tissues as he probed the channel it made in Doug's chest. He told Doug of the fever that had ravished him. He had done what he could to save the American. Now, he said with a smile, it looked as if Doug was going to survive both his wound and the treatment given for it. The man smiled and Doug realized he had made a small joke. He laughed appreciatively and the effort caused streaks of pain to shoot across his chest.

Then came the bad news. In a day or two he would be picked up by interrogators of the government of the Democratic Republic of Viet Nam—the northern communist nation. He was to be transferred to a POW camp, or a prison. The doctor was unsure which it would be. "You have been brave thus far, *Dai uy*. You have withstood much pain. Perhaps you will be able to continue your bravery after you are picked up and taken to a captive place. You will need bravery, for those who deal with you will not look kindly upon a man responsible for the destruction of an entire village." With those words, the physician and his interpreter left the medical hut, never to return. Worry now crinkled Andrews' brow. He had heard tales of the "interrogations" given allied prisoners by the NVA and he wanted no part of them. Terror of the unknown besieged him as he wondered what might become of him.

* * * * *

He slept. His dreams were colored in crimson. He heard again the rattle of rifle fire, the harsh noise of exploding grenades, the sound of flames crackling as they consumed bamboo huts, the anguished cries of children, the wails of women and old men, the shouts of angry soldiers. He saw blood soaking into the ground and again he heard the words of his unit's chaplain, Major Paul Eastley, preaching on the book of Genesis and outlining the feud between the two sons of Adam and Eve, and the envy Cain felt for Abel. He heard Eastley's words, "and after Cain had taken Abel's life, God spoke to him and said 'the voice of thy brother's blood crieth unto me from the ground.' And now art thou cursed from the earth.'" The blood of the inhabitants of Yen Song (3) surely also cried out. Why had he allowed this evil thing? Was he also now cursed? When he wakened, his cheeks were wet with tears and his breath came in sobs. When he had arrived in Viet Nam he had so wanted to be a good officer and conduct himself honorably, to make a difference, to guard the lives of the men assigned to him. He had failed in all three. The fruits of his weakness that day at Yen Song (3) were like the taste of bitter almonds on his tongue.

* * * * *

The old beat-up Ford pickup pulled to a stop in front of the medical hut. Two men got out. One was the driver who stood stretching beside the cab. The other seemed to be an officer of some kind, for the Vietnamese wounded and the medical personnel gave him great courtesy. The officer did not even look at Andrews, but spoke to two healthy men and pointed at the truck. Doug was taken from his pallet and frogmarched to the back of the vehicle. Over the bed was a camper top, its rear door open. The officer lowered the tailgate and thumbed Andrews into the back. There were no blankets, no straw on which he could lie. He crouched on the bare metal as the men returned to the cab, coughed the engine into life, and drove away.

From the very beginning it was a tortuous ride for Andrews. The truck rattled and shook, its wheels seeming to seek out every pothole in the nearly nonexistent roadway. His body thrown first one way and then another, it was only a matter of moments before the ride began to plague the soft, slowly healing tissues of the wound in Andrews' chest. He groaned. He cried out. He screamed in pain. The truck did not slow its pace nor did either of the men in front come back to try to alleviate his pain.

The trip was endless, continuing for many jolting hours as the miles peeled slowly away under the truck's wheels. Doug lapsed in and out of consciousness. During those brief painful moments when he could look around, Doug could see nothing along the roadway but jungle that sometimes even arched across the top of the trail, successfully hiding it from prying airborne eyes. They passed no villages, no hamlets, no discernible landmarks that Doug could imprint on his mind. He was totally disoriented knowing not even which of the cardinal points of the compass they followed. He only knew that he was too weak to attempt to escape and too far to expect any help from others. At about midday the truck stopped and the two men in front dismounted and unwrapped balls of sticky rice wrapped in banana leaves and began to eat their lunch. They offered Doug nothing, neither rice nor water. The officer did, however, finally deign to speak to him. *"Dai uy,* you will have to suffer greatly for the massacre at Yen Song (3). This I promise you."

* * * * *

During the ride that afternoon as the heaving and bouncing truck made its slow way along the road, Doug cried out repeatedly for relief from his pain. He was ignored by his captors. As the truck negotiated one particularly deep hole in the road, Doug's head was snapped back against the side rail of the vehicle's bed. His vision hazed, then reddened, then turned to black.

* * * * *

First Sergeant Harold Spruance laughed as he walked among the outlying buildings of Yen Song (3). Everywhere he looked he saw fearful and frantic people scrambling for safety. For the first time since his arrival in this war-torn country he was among people who were more frightened than he. It was exhilarating to have such power, to be able to panic others without effort. Two old mama-sans walked toward him, their eyes wide with fear, their arms held high in the air. He blinked his eyes and shook his head. His trigger finger tightened and he fired at the women. Four Vietnamese hiding in a family shelter in the hooch to his left suddenly panicked and fled for the dubious safety of the nearby rice paddies/ One was a young woman carrying her new-born child.

"By God, I'll show them," Harold screamed. He turned his sixteen on them and cut them down. He walked up to the crumpled bodies. The baby was still alive but crying from a hurt received while falling. Spruance fired. The wailing stopped.

* * * * *

The sky had just grown dark when the truck's engine stopped. Doug managed to look outside one of the camper's windows. He could barely make out a jungle compound constructed of bamboo and thatch, ringed by concertina wire. The doors to the camper were thrown open and Doug was dragged out. The driver supported his weight as he half-walked, half-carried the nearly delirious Andrews through the gate of the compound. He was thrown into a dark hooch inside which Doug could hear the rustling of geckos as they moved in the palm frond ceiling above him. He staggered around the room gazing into the blackness trying to find a bed to lie in. Nothing. He fell to the ground and slept.

At morning's first light, Andrews looked outside the one window in his hooch, trying to determine the lay-out of the compound. He saw again the concertina fence ring, but this time he was also able to see a guard tower at one corner of the camp. Presumably there were three others. He sighed. Then his eyes caught on a sight he had heard about but never seen. Here and there, hanging in suspended tiny cages made of bamboo, he saw other POWs trying to hold on to their miserable lives. He could hear their groaning as they roused from their stupors of the night to face the rigors of another day. Andrews knew such devices were called tiger cages—too low for prisoners to stand in, to narrow to lie down. It did not take many hours after being confined in such a place for a man's body to become transfigured with agony.

An angry voice called him from the doorway. Andrews turned and saw a guard holding out a bowl of what might have been soup. Doug took it gratefully and smiled at the guard who reached out and slapped him in the face, almost causing him to drop the bowl of gruel. After the guard left, Doug raised the bowl to his lips to drink, only then noticing the drowned body of a large Vietnamese cockroach

11

floating in the liquid. Fishing out the cockroach with a filthy fingertip, Andrews drank.

For some days Doug remained in that hut, unbothered by anyone, even the guards who reluctantly came periodically to give him rice, or bamboo shoots, or soup. In those days Doug's occasional examination of his chest wound showed that it slowly continued to heal. Yet he was afraid of another infection for the bandages had not been changed since he had been taken from the medical hut and now were a dirty grey, probably alive with microscopic organisms.

* * * * *

There came a day when he was taken from his hut. Still weak, Doug shambled along beside his guards. They brought him into a more substantial building, to a room in which the only furniture was a desk and one chair. Seated at the desk was a thin man wearing a rumpled uniform. Open before him on the desk lay a ledger which the man briefly consulted. He spoke.

"You are Douglas MacArthur Andrews. Is that correct?"

"Yes."

"You are charged with leading a massacre of the inhabitants of the hamlet of Yen Song (3). Is that correct?"

"Sir, the Geneva Convention requires that, as a prisoner of war, I need to tell you only my name, rank, and service number. I am Captain Andrews. My service number is 507-30-8821."

The interrogator's hand slapped down on the table top. The report was so sharp it startled Doug. "You are <u>not</u> a prisoner of war. You are a butcher. The articles of the Geneva Convention do not apply to you. In any case, we are not signatories to those articles. Thus no special treatment will be given you. You will be questioned until you admit that you are a butcher and ask for our forgiveness. Then, if you are lucky and if we believe you are sincere, we will have you shot. You are dismissed."

The guards hustled him from the room and back to his hooch. They pushed him, stumbling, inside. Doug sat hunched on the floor and his mind drifted back to that day at Yen Song (3).

* * * * *

Rick Carney looked into one of the bamboo huts and saw several people inside, huddled on the floor, their backs instinctively turned toward the door as if by that act they could protect themselves from the horrors that had come unbidden into their lives. Carney pulled the pins on two grenades, one after the other, watched the levers flip away, and rolled the fragmentation weapons across the dirt floor. Two explosions came, sound and flash. As he walked toward the next building there was only a muted low moaning from the ruined building behind him.

* * * * *

Once again, Doug stood in that barren room before the interrogator, warily watching his granite hewn features. "It is time for me to introduce myself to you. My name is Le Thuy Lam. You will soon learn that you can not come here from America and attack and murder my people with impunity. *Dai uy*, are you ready to confess to your crimes?" Doug stood at attention, mute, his eyes fixed on a spot just above the man's head.

"Are you ready to confess?"

Doug stood in silence.

The interrogator, what was his name? Lam!–cried out. "For murdering the Vietnamese people and making war against the Democratic Republic of Viet Nam you must be punished." He nodded to the two truncheon-carrying guards standing nearby. They stepped up to Doug and each slammed his club against his ribs on opposite sides. Doug cried out in pain and his knees buckled. It was as if a huge fist had slammed his entire body. He could never thereafter remember clearly the sequence of events. He turned his head to look at the guards who had violence in their eyes. The two swarmed over him, pummeling and kicking him. Doug felt a truncheon blow blast against his head. Consciousness exploded into brilliant lights which faded quickly into utter blackness.

* * * * *

The men with Skip Condon moved through Yen Song (3) rounding up groups of women and children. They shot men of fighting age on the spot. The others they herded toward a ditch that

13

ran along the north boundary of the hamlet. They put the captives under the close watch of Anderson and Doty. The two heavy weapons team soldiers aimed their M-60 at the captives. There were thirty of them. As Condon and the others walked back toward the center of the hamlet they heard the sound of an M-60 firing behind them. They continued on, wandering through the hamlet, firing their sixteens at those still scrambling to escape or cowering in some shelter. Gurtleff and Shores thumbed cigarette lighters into flame at each hooch they passed, setting the thatched structures on fire.

Smoke and flames roared skyward as house after house fell victim to the conflagration. Everywhere was noise and confusion. Weapons fired continuously. Hand grenades exploded as soldiers dropped them into family shelters or tossed them under the hooves of draft animals. Squads were so intermingled that they lost any semblance of unit cohesiveness. The mob rampaged on.

* * * * *

At *Ong* Lam's insistent order, Andrews rose shakily to his feet. Suffering from pain, tired, hungry, afraid, he found it was all he could do to keep his balance.

"Do you apologize to the Vietnamese people?" the officer asked. Doug stood silently, staring straight ahead, heart hammering in his chest, mind clouded with fear. Angered at his silence, Lam delivered himself of a brief lecture about the travesties the war had visited upon his countrymen. Doug's apprehension mounted. He tried to comfort himself by remembering his stateside escape and evasion survival training. He recalled being told that usually captors who punish and torture prisoners eventually give up on men who refuse to break, but continue their punishment so long as they believe there is any chance of success. Doug knew himself to be tough. He would endure whatever they might do to him. This he promised himself.

"Do you apologize?" Doug shook his head, determined to convince Lam that time spent on him was wasted.

The interrogator rapped out instructions to the guards. One stepped close to Andrews and slapped him, hard, with an open palm to the side of the face. Losing his balance, Andrews toppled to the floor and lay there grunting from the force of the landing. The guards hauled him to his feet.

"Do you apologize?"

Doug remained mute. Another hard slap, from the other guard, on the other side of his face. Once again he fell to the floor, smashing his head against the stone surface there. He started to groan but bit back his cry. *"By God these little bastards aren't going to have the satisfaction of hearing me complain."*

"Apologize!"

Another blow. Another fall. Another . . . and another. Doug kept his silence, staring groggily ahead. Another slap. Another demand for an apology. No acknowledgment. The tempo and strength of the blows and falls increased. Now each time Doug hit the floor the guards kicked him with booted feet in kidneys, stomach, groin, knees and head. One ground his heel into Doug's face, by now a bloody mass of beribboned flesh. But with set teeth and clenched jaw, Andrews managed to keep silent. No word would escape from his mouth–either of apology or pain.

The guards continued to hit his head, launching blows against his ears, ramming the heels of their hands under his jawbone and chin. Doug tried to roll as best he could with the blows, trying to protect his head by hunching his shoulders, concentrating on keeping his face devoid of expression.

Ong Lam finally gestured and the guards stepped back. For a moment or two Lam stared impassively at Andrews. Then he rose from his chair behind the desk, walked up to Doug, leaned close, and said, "You insult the Vietnamese people! I spit on you!" He spat a foul glob of mucous directly into Doug's face, and at last Andrews could take no more. His anger boiling over he spat a full measure of bloody froth back into Lam's face. The officer backed away, wiped his face, and spoke angrily to the guards. Doug knew things were about to get even worse than they had been, but he was certain that he was not going to give in.

The guards swarmed over him, holding his shoulders and arms. *Ong* Lam stood in front of him and smashed his fists into Doug's face

15

as hard as he could. Soon Doug's nose broke and claret spilled from it. Several teeth broke. Andrews could feel the slivers from them in his mouth. Once, when his jaw was slammed upwards and sideways, he felt the side of a molar break away.

Lam finally stepped away, his arms tired and hanging limply by his sides. Doug lay sprawled in the midst of a pool of blood, gasping for air, trying desperately not to break his vow of silence.

"Are you going to admit you are a butcher and apologize to the Vietnamese people?" Lam asked in a shrill voice.

Doug lay silent, watching as Lam picked up a bamboo club about three feet long and one and a half inches in circumference, the last few inches split into fourths. Lam gave a signal and the two guards grabbed Andrews and turned him onto his belly, one holding his arms outstretched while the other sat astride his legs.

"Apologize."

No answer.

Lam brought the club down hard across Doug's buttocks.

"Apologize."

Doug's mind gave the answer. *"I wouldn't say shit to you, you little prick."*

Another blow.

No sound.

Lam's demands for an apology became louder and more frequent. The guards strained to hold Doug as he writhed and arched his body in pain from the blows, pain that seemed to double with each strike. He was having trouble keeping his silence. His spirit did not want his tormentors to have the satisfaction of seeing him cry out in agony, but his flesh was weakening. The beating went on and on.

Finally Doug knew he could no longer keep the pain from showing. He lifted his head and turned it toward the wall, so that Lam could not see him grimacing, with tears streaming down his cheeks. He could see his own blood splattering on the nearby wall. So much blood had welled up on his buttocks that it was being forced through the cloth of his pants by the force of the blows. He was frightened now. He had never known such pain.

16

At last he screamed a long agonizing cry. Immediately Lam cast the rod aside, beckoned to the two guards and the three men walked from the interrogation room, leaving Doug's bloodied body, still writhing in pain, behind them. Doug lay trying to catch his breath and gather his wits. He was alone, in pain, and no one came. The dreadful certainty grew that Lam intended to leave him like this. He fought silently with his pain as long as he could. Then, sure he could no longer retain his sanity without doing so, he began screaming. He cried and pleaded for help. He slobbered. He gibbered. He agonized. He shrieked obscenities, damning to hell everyone he had ever known with particular emphasis upon Lam and the guards. He tried counting numbers. He prayed. He remembered his good friend Chaplain (Major) Paul Eastley who had helped him before in some difficult times, but where was he now? He cried out until his voice was gone. Then he lay in silence and in agony wondering how it was possible for man to inflict such pain on man. And then he remembered.

* * * * *

Doug walked drunkenly toward the ditch on the north side of Yen Song (3), for the first time in a year ignoring his surroundings. He saw the pile of bodies lying there. One young boy tried to drag himself from under the press of corpses. Andrews leveled his weapon at him and pulled the trigger. The boy's head exploded. "Filthy, slimy, putrid, miserable, stinking goddam gooks," he muttered. He walked back toward the settlement.

Everywhere could be heard the sound of firing, the crackle of flames, men's hoarse cries, the screams of women, children crying, the sound of explosions.

As he walked through the hamlet, Andrews found several wounded Vietnamese crouching in a homemade shelter under a hut. Two women held children. One little boy's arm bled profusely as his mother tried to staunch the flow of claret. Doug looked at them and saw only the mutilated body of Second Lieutenant Norman Crosse and the crumpled heap Leroy Johnson made on the ground. "You can't do that to my men," he snarled and fired his weapon.

Within forty minutes from the sound of the mortar explosion that killed Crosse, the once peaceful hamlet lay in smoke and ruins. Bodies of humans, animals and fowl lay contorted and still on the ground. War had brought peace to the land after all. The peace of death.

* * * * *

He lay there all that day and then through the night. His eyes were swollen shut and he could feel the rawness and swelling all across his face. His tongue was split and bleeding but he used it to feel the jagged destruction of broken teeth in his mouth. His lips and nostrils were caked with blood. His buttocks throbbed during all the hours of his exile.

He was determined not to yield and determined to survive. He knew that if he died, no one would ever know that it had been caused by mistreatment in this North Vietnamese jungle camp. The form of Nancy West swam before his eyes. He wanted desperately to be with her once again. By all that was holy, one day he would!

Late the next day *Ong* Lam and the two guards returned. No food was given him but Lam held a cup of brackish water to his swollen lips. Doug gasped and greedily sucked the liquid.

"You are a brave man, *Dai uy*, but it will do you no good. Since you will not confess and apologize to me, I am sending you to a place where you will one day willingly do so."

He gestured to the guards and they, grabbing Doug's arms, hauled him to his feet. Andrews screamed in pain. The blood from his buttocks had formed a huge scab that had adhered to the cloth of his trousers. The act of being pulled upright forced the scab and pants to partially separate and pain shot through his body. The guards pulled Andrews out of the building and over to the parking area of the camp. There a truck awaited. Two men stood beside it. One was obviously an officer, the other the driver. The driver smoked a cigarette until, seeing the approaching men, dropped it to the ground and ground out the coals with his heel.

The guards hustled Andrews to the rear of the vehicle and opened the tailgate. They picked him up and threw him into the truck's bed. As he collapsed on the floor, Doug realized that at least this time someone had thought to provide him with a thick layer of rice straw upon which he could sprawl. Lam had accompanied him on the trip to the truck.

"Remember, you are not a mistreated prisoner of war. You are a war criminal with no rights whatsoever. You came here to murder us and destroy our settlements. Your fate is now in the hands of the Vietnamese people. I think you will learn."

CHAPTER TWO

"For all his days are sorrows."–Ecclesiastes II: 23a

The truck jolted through the countryside for several hours. As the time passed, Captain Doug Andrews kept his eyes fixed on the landscape outside the vehicle. If he were ever to escape, it would be crucial to know something about his location, about the cardinal points of the compass, about streams and rivers, about crossed roadways, about hamlets and villages, about fields and dikes, about the size of the rural population in this area.

He was soon confused. Too much information crowded upon him, overpowering his weakened ability to concentrate. He was even unsure what part of Viet Nam he was traveling through save that the way chosen by the driver cut through thick triple canopy jungle. Was he above the 17th parallel and thus in "Indian" territory? Was he traveling through one of the many provinces below that line in which Viet Cong power held sway, denying control to the legitimate Republic of Viet Nam? Was he even in that third of the ancient land known as An Nam or had he been taken so far north he was now in Ton Kin? He knew but one thing for certain. The further north he was carried, the more difficult escape became.

Early morning gave way to noon. The truck did not stop. The hours of afternoon passed and still the vehicle maintained its way north. Finally at dusk the officer called a halt and he and the driver got out of the cab. They came to the rear, opened the tailgate and roughly hauled Doug out of the pickup. The driver handed him a bottle of water and Doug gulped it frantically. The officer pointed to the ground and Doug sat. He was given a banana leaf wrapped around a ball of sticky rice which he ate with relief. It was certainly not what he would have chosen but he realized that if he was to survive, he would have to eat whatever was available. Nothing should be allowed to overpower his taste buds.

When he finished eating his two captors tied his hands behind him, tied his ankles together and threaded the rope through both. Now hobbled, there was little chance that he would make any escape attempts that night. With his boot the officer pushed him over onto his side. The two Vietnamese then crawled into sleeping bags and slept. Night insects buzzed around Doug's filthy chest bandages, doing their best to crawl right into the wound. He lay for a long while listening to the night sounds. And then he slept.

* * * * *

At first light his captors kicked him awake and hustled him back into the truck. Bones aching from his night on the ground, Doug was relieved to once again collapse into the thick carpet of rice straw. The starter on the old truck ground and ground before the engine finally caught, running roughly for a moment or two before settling into a smoother rhythm.

"My mother, the war protestor and worker for peace. If she could only see me now," thought Doug. Then he realized that none of his family should have to bear the pain of seeing how badly he was hurt, how illy he had been treated. It was far better that they remain ignorant of his situation.

About mid-morning the truck driver drove his vehicle up to a substantial, solid-looking large stone building. Outside stood guards, weapons at the ready. The compound was ringed with concertina wire and guard towers reared above the scene. The officer came around the truck, lowered the tailgate, and surprised Doug by ordering him to climb out. Heretofore he had been manhandled in and out. It was some small relief to move gently so as not to aggravate his ruined buttocks and the rest of his aching body. Once on the ground he tried to stand at attention but was unable to do so. He stood hunched over, weak-kneed, nearly crying from the pain he felt.

The officer snapped his fingers and two armed guards soon materialized. Pointing toward the building, they urged Andrews into a slow walk. They entered through a heavy wooden door reinforced by iron bars and moved into a room that appeared to Andrews to be a copy of an American police station. He stood in a sizable open space before a high counter behind which sat a stern-looking Vietnamese man. On a standard behind him hung a red flag with a yellow five-pointed star emblazoned in the middle. It was, Doug realized with a sinking heart, the national flag of the communist Democratic Republic of Viet Nam. He was somewhere far north of the 17th parallel. There would be no American rescue attempt. Indeed, his brigade commander, Colonel Vernon "Savage" Moore, his battalion commander, Lieutenant Colonel Jeremiah Barrett, and even his good friend Captain Don Stoddard all probably believed him to be dead. If he was ever to see freedom again it would have to come through his own efforts.

* * * * *

Using rudimentary English the man behind the counter asked Andrews his name, his rank, his officer number, his age, his marital status, his length of time in service and asked him to identify the various cloth badges sewn to his uniform shirt. The questions seemed reasonable and Doug politely responded. The man then informed him that he would be questioned in a day or two by a man known for gaining eager cooperation from the prisoners who came there. He told Doug that the man, whose name was Colonel Cao Ba Thien, spoke excellent English for he had studied in the United States in earlier years at a school named Nebraska Wesleyan University, located somewhere in the middle of the plains country in a town named after an American president—Monroe? Adams? Roosevelt? He could not remember.

"Colonel Thien will be your good friend if you cooperate with him." The desk sergeant smiled at Doug revealing gums lacking several teeth, and those that remained were stained with betel nut. Andrews ducked his head in acknowledgment of what he had been told.

He was led away, down a wide corridor on the floor of which were occasional brown spots. Doug shuddered. He did not even want to know what those spots were or how they had gotten there. The guard who escorted him made a right turn at an intersection of corridors, counted off three doors, and put a key into the lock of the fourth. The door swung open and he pushed Andrews inside. He closed and locked the door. The room was dim and it took Doug's

23

eyes some moments to adjust. He looked around. The room was small, about eight feet by eight feet. An iron cot was bolted to the wall. A thin blanket lay on top of a mattress stuffed with rice straw. A bucket sat in one corner, reeking of human waste. A food bowl and chopsticks lay on the floor beside the bed. That was all. This was now his world for the foreseeable future.

* * * * *

He tried to lie down gently on the cot, but each movement brought the hurts of his beating back into focus. Finally he was as comfortable as possible and he slept. He awakened rudely. His body itched everywhere. He frantically scratched and scratched. Then he realized. The rice straw mattress was filled with lice. As he scratched he saw cockroaches entering and leaving his waste bucket and in the walls he could hear the patter of rats' feet as they made their way along internal tunnels.

"Well, for damn sure this isn't the Hilton," he grumbled. But even with the filth and squalor of his cell, he remained glad that no one was beating him. He lay there in those night hours, rubbing his itching skin and listening to the heavy silence. He wondered how he could stand up to being in a louse-infested cell. His skin had been susceptible to irritation ever since his arrival in Viet Nam. At one point, along with malaria and stomach parasites, his inflamed skin had sent him to the hospital. That was where he had met Nancy. At the thought of her, he smiled slightly through bruised, swollen and cracked lips. Then he heard a series of tapping noises. At first he thought they might have been knocking water pipes, but they were too regular for that. He wondered what caused them. And again he slept.

* * * * *

He dreamed. Only a few feet away lay a tangled pile of corpses. From nearby came the agonized bellow of a water buffalo. It stood with its head hanging low, mucous dropping in a long bloody string from its mouth and nose. Blood from other wounds dripped steadily onto the ground. Doug walked on. On all sides, thatch and bamboo hooches crackled, sparks shooting up from their ruined remains. He

24

stood at the ditch and looked down upon the contorted bodies lying there and the nearby sprinkles of expended 7.62-mm brass. He reached down and picked up one of the empty cartridge cases. Suddenly he found himself in Hawaii on R & R with Nancy, sitting at a restaurant table, saying to her, "You know, Nancy, I've been in Viet Nam too long." How right he had been. He stared dully at the pall of smoke that hovered over Yen Song (3).

* ** * *

He awoke with a start, his mind reeling from the horror that possessed it when he slept. The quality of light in the cell had changed. Now it was just a little brighter. Thus a new day had begun. He was thirsty and hungry. Despite the fact that he had not eaten since that ball of sticky rice had been given him during the trip to this prison, his bowels churned and he quickly moved to the waste bucket, pulled down his trousers and emptied a burst of liquid diarrhea into it. He looked around for something to use to clean himself but could find nothing. With a sigh he pulled up his pants, knowing that the remnants of the acidic discharge would soon begin to eat away at his tender skin.

Noises in the corridor caught his attention. He listened. Voices, coming closer, stopping periodically, probably at other cells. Doug could hear the sound of metal. Then the voices were outside his cell. The slot opened and a bowl of rice with what might have been a chunk or two of chicken was pushed through the opening to him. He found his chopsticks and sat on the edge of his cot eating the rice. It certainly was not the chicken and yellow rice his mother made so well. This seemed to have been prepared by a truck mechanic or someone else who had never before put a meal together. Still it was food and Doug ate hungrily. As he did so, once again he heard the mysterious tapping in the walls of his cell.

An hour or so after finishing his meal, Doug heard a key slide into the lock on his cell door. It swung open to reveal a guard who beckoned to him. Doug rose carefully so as not to exacerbate his wounds and stepped into the corridor. The guard pointed and Doug

25

followed his finger, trying his best to walk normally. He did not succeed.

They walked through a succession of corridors, finally arriving at a room that was bathed in light. Once again there was a desk, its legs bolted to the floor. Behind it sat a comfortable looking desk chair with padded seat, back and arms. Rows of recessed electrical bulbs in the ceiling allowed no corner of the room to hide in shadow. In front of the desk sat two high stools. Doug looked toward the ceiling and saw attached to a beam there a large pulley. A pleasant faced, unsmiling man sat at the desk. From the beginning, even before he spoke, Doug knew he was in trouble.

"I am Lieutenant Colonel Cao Ba Thien. I am thirty-five years old. My home is Hoi An, a fishing village on the coastline of the South China Sea a little south of Da Nang. The puppet government controls that area. My wife and children remain there. I have not seen them in four years and miss them very much. The illegitimate southern government does not know what I do. It remains ignorant of the fact that I hold a commission in the North Vietnamese Army. So far as it is concerned, I am dead.

"I understand that you are from Nebraska. You will then know where I received my university degree. I attended a Methodist school, Nebraska Wesleyan University in Lincoln, Nebraska. And you, sir, I understand, were born and raised in a small town some one hundred miles north and west, the town of Central City. Am I correct?"

Andrews nodded. "Yes, sir. That is correct."

Thien continued. "I enjoyed my time in America. I made several very good friends. And then your government decided to come here and pillage my nation. And did so after we had spent many long, bloody years after the end of World War II fighting the French efforts to once again make us into a colony. After Dien Bien Phu we finally drove them out, only to have the United States replace them. Your government recognized the illegitimate southern so-called republic headed by the criminal Ngo Dinh Diem. You and other soldiers like you have laid waste to my country. You have poisoned our vegetation. You have bombed us everywhere. You have killed our soldiers and our civilians. Your artillery has made it difficult even for a poor farmer to work his rice fields or tend to his buffalo. You have killed our women. Our children. Those things are bad enough, but they are the sort of thing that happens in wartime.

"But you, Captain, are a special case. You brought the men of your platoons to Yen Song (3). A company commander is supposed to control his men through discipline and example. You failed. According to this report here"–he gestured at a paper laying in front of him–"you not only failed to exert discipline to keep your soldiers in line, but you led them in the attack upon Yen Song (3). You set the example, Captain. You personally killed babies and women and old men. You, sir, are a criminal. You have been told this before. I want to remind you. You are not a prisoner of war, and we have many of those. You are a criminal, a butcher, without shame, without morals, without conscience. And you will come to regret what you did. Not only will you regret it, but you will publicly apologize for your criminal acts against the people of Viet Nam. You will be so filled with remorse that you will <u>ask</u> to speak out on our behalf and against the land of your birth. You will expose those above you as uncaring egotists, more interested in furthering their own careers than in fighting a war."

All this was said in a quiet, conversational manner. Colonel Thien continued.

"When I was at Wesleyan, I studied philosophy. I learned about the western world's great theologian, St. Augustine. I discovered that it was he who first found a way for Christians to fight in wars on behalf of the Roman empire. Did you know that, Captain?"

"No, sir, I did not."

"Augustine saw the Vandals invading the empire, occupying large tracts of it, ever moving toward control of Rome. They crossed the great sea–Romans called it *mare nostrum*–our sea–and moved along Africa's northern tier of land. Finally they threatened Carthage, where Augustine held sway as bishop of the church. They besieged the city. Augustine did not believe that prayers alone would serve any

27

purpose. And so he worked out certain rules for what has ever since been called a 'just war.'

"For him a war–to be just–must be declared by a legitimate government. It must be entered upon as a last resort, after all other remedies for existing problems have been exhausted. The cost of the war must be weighed against the possible benefits. It must be fought in a virtuous cause. It must be fought according to certain rules, openly acknowledged. Civilians are not to be harmed and the conflict must occur only between the two opposing armies. Prisoners must not be harmed. The enemy must be given an opportunity to repent. And any peace treaty must resolve the issues that brought the two sides to war initially.

"That, Captain, is a just war. Your world so enjoyed Augustine's theory that it became part of international law under Hugo Grotius. Lip service is still given to it, even in General Westmoreland's cards listing the 'Rules of Engagement' which are given to every soldier arriving in Viet Nam.

"You, sir, disobeyed those rules. You <u>led</u> your soldiers into Yen Song (3) and allowed them, with your help, to rampage through the community. My sources tell me that you killed all but three of the inhabitants. Those few persons were able to escape into the jungle without being seen.

The Viet Cong 48th Local Force Battalion was able to punish your unit. I believe your men used up all their ammunition before they discovered that the 48th was marching against them. One after another, they were killed by our men in just retribution for their bloody, criminal acts. You were the last to 'die.' One of our soldiers–you knew him as a *chieu hoi*, but he actually holds a commission at the same rank as you in the North Vietnamese Army–found you hiding under a dead man and, so angry was he, that he shot you in the chest. Only then did he come to his senses and realize that you could be more valuable to us alive than dead. He it was who took you to death's door and then pulled you back to life.

"Now I ask you, Captain. Are you willing to confess your sins, to apologize to the Vietnamese people, and to speak out against the criminal conduct of your nation?"

"Sir, I am a soldier. I can not do that."

Colonel Thien smiled. "Before long you may change your mind, Captain. Others in the past have tried to refuse, but, without exception, they have all come to see that it was in their best interest to cooperate with me.

"Have I been correct with you this day?"

"Yes, Sir."

"Then would you please sign this statement saying that I have treated you humanely?" He pushed a sheet toward Andrews and held out a pen. Doug picked up the paper and read it. It said what Thien had told him. He took the pen and scrawled his name on the page and returned it to the colonel.

The colonel had the last word. "I realize that our accommodations here are not the best, but you are lucky to have any at all. By rights you should be moldering in a grave outside Yen Song (3). Every breath you take is a gift to you from the Vietnamese people. Return now to your cell. We will speak again soon and I hope you come to your senses and do what I ask."

He nodded to the guard who had brought Doug from his cell. The two retraced their steps until once more Andrews was securely locked in his tiny cell. He sat on the cot, listened to the knocking in the walls, and worried. What, he wondered, did Colonel Thien have in store for him? After a time sleep possessed him.

* * * * *

He came out of the hamlet on the south looking for his troops. Then he saw them a hundred yards or so ahead, clustered together holding their weapons as a line of Viet Cong soldiers walked toward them firing their rifles. A mortar round fell into the group of his men, wiping life from their bodies in an instant of time. Enemy troops walked among them, occasionally snapfiring their rifles. What had happened? Doug did not know. His men were dead but there was no reason he should volunteer to join them so he dropped to the ground

29

and rolled over against the corpse of one of the men from the ruined hamlet. Andrews rubbed his hand in the wounds of the bloody body beside him and then wiped his hand on his uniform and face. Then he lay still, feigning death.

He heard a sound and opened his eyes slightly. The battalion *chieu hoi* was walking toward him, now carrying an AK-47 rifle whereas earlier he had been unarmed. Doug wondered how he had gotten a weapon. The captain lay as still as possible. Grass stems, cool and sweet, touched his cheek. An ant walked across the back of his hand, its tiny feet tickling him in their passage. The *chieu hoi* walked closer and then stopped. He spat out a stream of rapid tonal Vietnamese. He must have said something about his own name for Andrews heard him say "Tyne." He lay utterly still.

Then Le Qui Thanh kicked him savagely in the side and Doug could not contain the grunt that escaped him. The last thing Andrews noticed was a sudden sound of light and heat and unbelievable fury. Pain blossomed in his chest. And then there was nothing.

* * * * *

Unchanging days passed. Andrews ate the meager food given him and drank the small amount of water allowed him. He used the waste bucket until the smell became overwhelming and the bucket overflowed. Only then did a guard take it away and empty it. Doug continued upon occasion to hear the tapping in the walls and he spent much time trying to figure out what caused it.

He learned that life in the prison was lived by the gong. There was a get-up gong at 0600 hours; a chow gong at 1000 signifying that prisoners were about to receive a meager helping of food. At 1600 in the afternoon came the dinner gong and at 2100 hours came the go-to-bed gong. It was to those dissident noises that Doug patterned his days. He spent most of his waking hours considering possible means of escape from the prison. Then came a day unlike those that preceded it.

Andrews slowly came to weary wakefulness as a hand continued to shake his shoulder. He opened his eyes and looked up. The door to his cell had banged open and two guards entered. One now stood

30

beside the cot roughly shaking him, ordering him to his feet. When he did not move with the speed they wanted, they hauled him upright and, with one gripping each arm, hustled Doug out of his cell and down the same corridors as he had trod some days ago when he had met Colonel Cao Ba Thien. They took him into the same interrogation room, still lit brightly, still with one desk and chair, still with two three-legged stools, still with suspicious brown discolorations on the floor. Doug stood quietly before the empty desk, wondering what was next. He was soon to learn.

Colonel Thien entered the room and took his place behind the desk. He addressed his prisoner.

"Captain, we have given you time to consider. Are you now ready to confess that you are a butcher and to ask publicly for forgiveness from the Vietnamese people? Are you ready to tell the world that the United States is here unjustly and without cause?"

His heart in his throat, Andrews replied. "Sir, my name is Douglas MacArthur Andrews. I am a captain in the United States Army. My service number is . . . ."

One of the guards smashed a truncheon into his ribs. Andrews fell to the floor gagging. As he lay there helpless, one guard slipped a loop of clothesline rope around one of his arms, just above the elbow. Standing on the arm, the guard pulled and cinched the rope until it could not have been made any tighter. In this manner he wound several such loops around the arm while his fellow guard did the same to Doug's other arm. With the circulation thus cut off, Doug soon found that he had lost all feeling below both elbows; he could neither feel nor move his hands and fingers.

Colonel Thien watched this impassively.

Then one guard stood in the middle of Andrews' back while the other began drawing his elbows together behind his back. A person's elbows do not easily come together in such a way. Both guards dedicated themselves to this work of defying nature and finally accomplished their task by dislocating Doug's shoulders. He screamed with the pain.

When the elbows were tied tightly together, Doug was made to balance himself on top of a three-legged stool which had been placed precariously on top of the other such stool, putting him some five feet above the level of the stone floor. It was all he could do to keep his balance. His apprehension mounted. Then, losing his balance atop the stool he tumbled to the floor. One guard kicked him several times as the other once again replaced the fallen stools.

It was hard to balance on the stool, his wounded buttocks still painful. As he tried to remain there, he felt increasing pain in his arms, shoulders, and chest cavity. His chest, he knew, hurt due to the bullet wound there. His arms and shoulders ached because of the ropes tied around his upper arms that then tied his elbows behind his back. The pain was intense.

Colonel Thien smiled at him, rose from his chair and left the room. Now Doug was alone with the two guards. One went behind him and let out the ropes binding his shoulders until the elbows were about two inches apart. Then both men left the interrogation room. The loosening of the bonds had relieved the pain slightly. Doug hoped he could work the ropes still looser, but his hands were useless, swollen to the size of cantaloupes. Neither hands nor fingers gave the slightest response to commands from his brain. They had begun to turn black and hung swollen and useless. Doug fell to the floor and lay there groaning. A guard charged back into the room, angrily pulled Doug once more into a sitting position on the stool. He hit him several times in the face and indicated he was not to try to get off the stool, nor to sleep.

Each time he sagged and fell from his stool a guard would appear and pull him upright again. He sat in that room all that day and all through the following night. He prayed that he might die. He could not take much more of this. And what was the use of trying to hang on to life? It would be better for it all to be over.

Mosquitoes filled the air around him, swarming over and around him, adding to the intensity of his misery. He had to keep his bloodied head constantly moving against his shoulders in a vain attempt to wipe away those insects. He worried about rats feasting on his ruined flesh. How could he keep them away if they came hungrily in the night? He shuddered, and even that slight movement fired the pain in his body. He worried about his thirst which burned with intensity. He worried about infection setting in upon the open wounds covering his body. His strength ebbed as his terror grew. All through those long hours Doug sat on his bloody striped buttocks.

As morning of the second day dawned, a guard entered the room and removed the ropes from his arms, leaving behind a cup of water and some watery gruel. Doug had never tasted anything quite so good as that dirty water and greasy, thin soup. He gulped them down in huge draughts, despite the clumsiness of his bloated hands which could hardly hold the dishes. For the most part his arms flopped around uselessly, like alien limbs attached to his body.

After a few minutes he began to wish that they really did not belong to him, for as blood began to force its way back through his forearms and into his hands, he learned of still a new agony. At length, the vessels once again filled with the flow of blood, the pain began to ebb.

At about midmorning Colonel Thien reentered the interrogation room and took his place behind the desk. He looked pleasantly at Andrews. He spoke.

"Captain, are you now ready to cooperate?"

"Sir. My name is Douglas MacArthur Andrews . . . ."

Thien gestured to the two guards, one of whom held a coil of rope. They grabbed Andrews and threw him onto his stomach so that they could reaffix the rope tightly to his arms. It did not take long and pain returned to Andrews' upper torso with a vengeance.

The long tail of the rope binding his elbows was then passed up and around the pulley fastened to the ceiling beam. The guards began pulling it taut. When all slack was gone from the rope, the guards gripped it and strained downward, hoisting Doug toward the ceiling. A scream ripped from his mouth as his arms and dislocated shoulders supported his dangling weight. He was pulled higher, until his toes no longer touched the floor. It was not possible for him to relieve any of his weight. Scream after scream filled the air of the room.

Doug could not believe this new pain that shrieked through every fiber of his being, penetrating and clinging from the top of his head to his toes. There was no getting used to it, for it got worse with every passing instant. Doug knew that shortly his shoulders would tear away from his torso. The guards pulled him higher, until his neck almost touched the pulley. They released their grip. Doug plunged toward the floor. Just before he reached that point, the guards snubbed the rope, stopping Doug's fall short. The jolt caused joint after joint to stress, some to separate. He cried out over and again in desperation.

He was pulled back high enough that his toes could not touch the floor. The three Vietnamese walked out of the room, leaving Doug dangling in the air behind them, his body twisting and contorting in spasmodic writhings while his voice pealed out again and again for succor, until it too became weak and hoarse. Doug was now so full of pain and the memory of it and the worry about more future pain that he quivered and shook, so hoarse from screaming and crying that he could no longer speak.

Colonel Thien and his men walked back into the room. It was Thien himself who loosened the rope holding Doug in the air. He fell suddenly to the stone paving, to lie there gagging in pain and horror, vomit filling his mouth and airways.

"Apologize!"

After a pause the colonel once again made his demand.

"Apologize!"

With terrible slowness, in sounds so muted they could hardly be understood, Doug found voice: "I apologize to the Vietnamese . . . people . . . and . . . to you, for . . . being . . . a butcher and . . . a criminal of the . . . United States."

Colonel Thien smiled down at him.

"There now, Captain. That wasn't so hard, was it?"

The two guards picked up Andrews and carried him back to his cell, threw him inside and slammed the door shut. Just before he lost consciousness, Doug heard a knocking in the walls.

* * * * *

The gongs continued to mark the passage of time. A new day came. Another and another. Slowly Doug regained a little strength and began to do what exercises he could in the tiny space that was his allotment in life. Those feeble efforts brought home to him how savagely he had been used. He could not stand upright. He could not walk without shambling. Every bowel movement was liquid. His kidneys still ached. Some of his ribs were, he knew, badly broken so that he could hardly draw a deep breath. He had a constant headache from having been kicked in the head. His nose, broken so badly, was slowly healing but Doug could tell that it was now puffy and crooked. But he was not called back to be interrogated by Colonel Cao Ba Thien. And for that Andrews was grateful. He prayed–yes, he prayed (Chaplain Eastley would be proud of him)–that he would never see the man again. Doug did not know whether he could live through another session with the man. The last time his heart beat so wildly he was sure he was going into cardiac arrest.

Wondering about the noises in the walls occupied much of his time. They seemed sometimes to have a rhythm. One wall would sound for a moment and then fall silent, only for the knocking to start over in another wall. One day, having laid on his cot listening, he tried an experiment. He lifted his food bowl and banged it tentatively against his wall. The knocking stopped. Then it began again, in all three of the inner three walls of his cell. He banged back. The knocking increased in intensity. He thought now that perhaps the noises were caused by inmates in other cells trying to communicate with one another. Were they now also trying to contact him? The sounds were, however, meaningless to him. This went on for some time until Doug tired of the distraction. He laid his bowl on the floor and went to sleep.

The rainy season ended and the walls of Doug's cell which had dripped condensation began to dry. He hardly even noticed the reek from his waste bucket any longer. Sometimes guards would come with a fresh supply of rice straw and throw it on the floor of his cell so he could renew the stuffing in his pallet. He still heard the rats and saw the geckos and scratched his inflamed skin continuously. He hated the lice with all his being but had found no way to rid himself of the little vermin. Still no one came to take him for another interrogation. He continued to pray daily that he would have the strength to survive whatever might come. He wondered about one change in prison routine. Heretofore the food cart came down the corridor and the food was pushed through the slot in his door by guards, two of which worked together. Now, occasionally, he caught a glimpse of a sole prisoner doing that work, unattended by any guard. Occasionally one man disappeared for days or weeks and was replaced by still another prisoner. "They must be trustees," Doug thought.

There came a day when one of the trustees paused at his door, shoved a hand through the slot and beckoned him with a finger. Doug came close, bent over and peered out. A nervous trustee thrust a piece of paper at him. "Take this. Memorize it. Then destroy it. The others want to be able to talk to you." And he was gone.

His eyes now used to the dim light in which he lived, Doug sat on his cot and bent over, the better to see what was written on the paper. It was a simple code.

	1.	2.	3.	4.	5.
1.	A	B	C	D	E
2.	F	G	H	I	J
3.	K	L	M	N	O
4.	P	R	S	T	U
5.	V	W	X	Y	Z

Doug noted that there was no "Q" but thought that the sound made by that letter could as easily be made by a "K" and the letter had probably been omitted for that reason. But what did the two series of numbers one through five mean? Perhaps he could find out. Now he listened to the rappings in the walls with new intensity. He noticed that the sounds came in succession. Sometimes a one, followed by a pause. Or a three or five or two or four. After that pause came another series of raps ranging from one to five. Finally Doug believed he understood. The first raps indicated the column, the second located the needed alphabet letter.

He listened, trying to learn whether his theory made sense.

Two knocks, followed by two knocks. A "B." Five raps followed by five more. An "E." A longer pause, then the noise began again. Three raps and then four. The letter "S." Four and then four more. "T." Two and four. "R." Five and three. "O." Four and three. "N." Two and two. "G." Someone had just told him to "be strong." Someone knew he was in the prison. Someone cared about his welfare. Someone wanted to help. It had been a long time since Doug had spoken to anyone. Now, in his exultation, he croaked "hallelujah!" Quickly committing the code to memory, Andrews chewed up the paper and then swallowed it. Now even a surprise inspection of his cell–although there had never been one–would reveal nothing.

Each new day now became more exciting as he used his newfound code to talk to other prisoners. Messages were short and simple. Names were exchanged. Unit designations were shared. Courage was urged. Resist torture as long as one could bear. Indeed, resistance was ordered. Doug learned that a chain of command existed within these walls. The highest ranking officer was a lieutenant colonel, a man named Jerry Corley. He had designated the next ranking officer as his second in command. The two together had chosen a staff from among the remaining prisoners. The North Vietnamese who ran this prison may not have realized it, but their prisoners had formed a resistance movement.

Doug learned to simplify the code so as to say more in less time. Words were abbreviated. Some letters stood for entire thoughts. He was told that the code was widespread throughout the prison. Inmates who were allowed to be outside to sweep the compound moved their brooms in coded ways. In the infirmary they coughed signs to one another. When necessary they could blink messages using the code. Or tap their fingers or feet. Such efforts gave them a sense of solidarity. But those more familiar expressions of the code were not for Captain Douglas MacArthur Andrews. Others might be able to have limited time outside the walls of the prison building. Very occasionally they were even allowed limited contact with one another. But, on orders from Colonel Cao Ba Thien, Doug Andrews was forced to remain in his cell, week after week, month after month, with only the raps of other prisoners to keep him company. And then one day it all changed.

* * * * *

It was evening meal time. Andrews could hear the orderly coming down the corridor handing out ladles of food, carelessly dumped into waiting bowls. The man stopped outside Doug's cell. A key turned in the lock. A figure stepped inside. As the man turned to relock the door behind him, Doug's breath caught in his throat. He would recognize that figure anywhere, not needing even to see his face. But it couldn't be. The man he now saw was long since left for dead in the jungle near the enemy bunker more than a year ago, accidentally shot by Rafael Jesus Terife de Palenque, one of his own men, during an attempted attack on that enemy stronghold. It was impossible! But there, standing in his cell was his good friend Jan Szigmond.

CHAPTER THREE

"Let not your heart be troubled."–John XIV: 1

Nancy West lay comfortably in his arms. She knew that tonight Jonathan Diedrich would propose to her. They had eaten earlier at an Italian restaurant and then had driven to this lookout above the city. They had parked and he had taken her in his arms. She looked out at the myriad of lights shining below. Each point of light seemed special to her. Each seemed to be saying, It's time to go on. It's time to put Doug into the back of my mind. It has been more than two years since we buried him. I still love him with all my heart, but it is my memory of him that I love. You can't really love a dead man.

She had known Jonathan for nearly a year. He was a pharmaceutical salesman and they had met at Brooke Army Hospital at Fort Sam Houston in San Antonio where she was stationed. He enjoyed telling her that he came that day to the hospital to call on physicians and instead lost his heart to the beautiful ward nurse on 4-E. She blushed the first time he said it, but as he repeated it on later occasions it seemed nice to her that he had felt that way and his saying the words always brought a smile to her lips. On that very first meeting he had asked her for a date and for some strange reason she said she would go out with him. Even as she told him that, her heart beat wildly as part of her mind told her that it was wrong, that she loved Doug, that at their last meeting in Hawaii she had promised to love him always.

Now, ten months later, she found herself drawn to Jonathan, always easy in his presence, missing him when he was not with her. Yet she was also certain that she did not love him in the way that he deserved. He was convenient. Fun. Nice looking. Strong. Persuasive. He had asked her to move in with him, but she had refused. Doug was part of the reason. Another was a fateful liaison that had happened before she met Doug when a man she loved dumped her cruelly and without warning. They had lived together for almost a year, and then he was gone, taking her virginity with him. For a time she was heartbroken. Then that eased into simple bitterness. That eventually resolved itself into her determination to remain remote from romance, unapproachable. She was determined not to let anything of the sort happen again. And then she met Doug while he recuperated from malaria, intestinal parasites and a skin fungus at her station field hospital in Viet Nam. All her resolutions about men disappeared when she tended to his care and they began talking. She wanted to know him better. She needed to be his friend. Then they met during his Hawaiian R & R and the week together in Honolulu was filled with laughter, romance, and beauty. Before he returned to Viet Nam he presented her with a beautiful engagement ring. The stone was more than a carat. When he gave it to her he pledged his love for her would last always. Held in his arms, she returned his vow.

But now he was dead. Buried in a closed casket service. Moldering in his grave, or at least what was left of him, for the Viet Cong had savagely mutilated his body. Gone for two years. How long must she grieve? Then Jonathan had come into her life, and she was glad for it. After he began seeing her, the nights were no longer lonely. The tears that soaked her pillow dried. Then he frightened her with his invitation to live together. She had only been intimate with two men in her life. She finally said "No," and Nancy believed that if Jonathan loved and treasured her, then he would be willing to wait–but wait for what? What was she to do?

She started to nestle deeper into his arms but instead found him pushing her upright so he could look at her. Jonathan reached into his pocket and pulled out a ring box, opened it, and held it toward her. "Nancy, I would be pleased if you would marry me. This is a symbol of my love for you." He placed it on her ring finger. She looked at it and found she could hardly breathe. Then the tears started and became deep, racking sobs that tore at her. The ring was beautiful. Jonathan was special. But he wasn't her Doug and that was almost more than she could bear.

Her tears upset Jonathan. He took her into his arms again and held her close. He cupped her left breast in his hand and whispered, "Don't cry, sweetheart. Just tell me that you love me."

The words were torn from her heart. "I do love you, Jonathan. But life isn't fair. I was dumped by one man, another died on me, and I wonder what will happen with you? How long before I am alone again?" And she bowed her head and with her hair hanging loose about her face, she wept.

* * * * *

Chaplain (Lieutenant Colonel) Paul Eastley, dressed in civilian clothes, walked the streets of his home town, Central City, Nebraska. It was the first time he had been here in two years, when he had officiated at the funeral of Captain Douglas MacArthur Andrews, scion of one of the most important families in the community. Now he was back home again. Yesterday he had laid his ninety-one year old mother to rest beside her husband who had passed away decades before. Now he was the only one of the Eastley family left. His poor mother had been in failing health for two years, and had spent most of that time in the long-term care facility at Litzenberg Hospital. He had flown in to see her on several occasions but she had usually been unresponsive.

It had broken his heart to see this proud woman curled in her bed in the fetal position. She had once been so strong. She had milked cows and tended sheep and weeded gardens and canned produce and fed harvest crews and cut firewood and did all the things that farm wives did when she was young. After the death of his dad, Paul recalled his mother moving into town, working at whatever was available. Cleaning houses for others, doing washing and ironing for those women who saw fit not to do their own. Cleaning pheasants and ducks for hunters. Cutting up chickens at the cold storage plant. Then she got a job as a bakery clerk, and then as a restaurant waitress. Finally she became night clerk at the Merrick hotel, on Main Street. She had worked steadily until she was eighty. Why? "I just always wanted to see if I could do that." When she got too old to hold that job she served as relief clerk at the Central City Motel. Even after she finally retired she regularly walked from her home, across the street

41

from the high school, to various points all over the downtown area as necessity demanded. She wanted always to be busy and so for some years served as the trip organizer for the local senior citizens group. She quit, she once told Paul, when those in the group all seemed to her to be such "kids."

Then she began falling. Small strokes. Constantly bruised and cut. Unsteady on her feet. Sometimes confused and unsure where she was. Sleeping more. Content to remain safely at home in her recliner rather than venturing out from the house. Now she kept contact with the outside world through her telephone. Then that became too much for her to cope with and Paul reluctantly placed her in the long term care facility. His own life and his choice of careers prevented him from taking her into his own home to care for her. Now she was gone forever. He had been at Fort Stewart, Georgia when he had been notified that she would not last many more hours. He flew to Atlanta and then to Omaha where he rented a car, hurrying against her last hours. When he arrived at the hospital he learned that she had died some hours earlier. He put his head on her chest and his arm across her body and cried like a child.

"I'm sorry I couldn't get here in time, Mom," he sobbed. "I love you so much."

Two days later on a blustery March day Edith Eastley was laid to rest beside her husband at Bureau Cemetery, across the road from Pierce Chapel, some fifteen miles north of Central City. After the ceremony, Paul stood looking at the Eastley plot. His grandmother and grandfather, his father and mother, all now lay there in the soil of Nebraska.

* * * * *

Chaplain (Lieutenant Colonel) Paul Eastley, still wearing civilian clothing, stood in front of Bested's Store at the intersection of Main Street and 17th Avenue. He watched heavy traffic flow along Main Street, part of U.S. Highway 30, once known as the "Lincoln Highway," and cynics scolded that "it had not been repaired since Lincoln built it!"

Paul debated what he should do next. He had extended his stay in Central City for two reasons. He might see old school friends. He wanted to pay his respects to the Andrews' family. He had not seen them in the two years since he had buried their son on that cold, cold winter day. It was early in the day. Perhaps he would go into the donut shop next to Bested's and have coffee and a donut.

His thoughts were interrupted by the sound of a friendly voice speaking his name.

"Paul! Paul Eastley!"

He turned to look and saw his old friend and schoolmate Cecil Currey standing there.

"How the hell are you Paul? Wups. I guess I should watch my language now that I am talking to a man of the cloth."

"Don't be silly, Ceec," Paul replied and reached out and hugged his friend. "I have not only heard worse. I have <u>said</u> worse. When you go to Viet Nam you begin using words you had only vaguely heard of before. What brings you to town? You don't live here anymore. I don't live here. Yet here we meet on Main Street."

"Well, I know what brought you to town, Paul. I've seen the notices around town in the stores about your Mom's funeral. She was a good woman, Paul, and I want you to know that I am really sorry that you lost her. As for me, I drove up from Lincoln to see my sister. Do you remember her? Ilene Good. Married to Merle Good. He farms for Lee Ferris and they live out in the old college section."

"Yeah, Ceec. Thanks for your sympathy. And sure, I know Ilene and Merle."

Changing subjects, Paul said, "What is this I hear about you having become an author?"

Currey shrugged. "I got lucky, I guess. When they hired me at Nebraska Wesleyan I told them I planned on writing books and the president said that was exactly the sort of person the school needed. Now I have two under my belt. Both on aspects of the life of Benjamin Franklin. More on the way someday, but I think I will change subjects. Have said about all I want to about him. Since I'm in the Nebraska National Guard I think I will begin writing military history."

43

Cecil punched Paul on the arm. "But what's this I have been hearing about you? A lieutenant colonel? Two purple hearts? A silver star? The Nonpareil even reported that, singlehandedly, you captured an enemy officer using only a machete. It sounds to me like you are living pretty dangerously. Chaplains aren't supposed to get medals like that. They are to stay back in their chapels and come out only on Sundays." He smiled.

"That wouldn't work for me, Ceec," Paul replied. "I have always got to stay with the men of whatever unit I am assigned to. And sometimes that has been a little dangerous. Hey. Let's go in the donut shop and talk awhile." And they did."

As they took their seats, Currey said "Paul, if you keep on this way, getting promotions and medals, you might become Chief of Army Chaplains one day."

"Not a chance, Ceec. In fact when the Chief learned that I had captured that guy he wanted to throw me out of the chaplaincy. He called me in and said that chaplains don't do that sort of thing. Nor, he said, do they earn silver stars. So I have those black marks on my records, and Chiefs or future chiefs are so politically minded that they strive never to do or say anything that might keep them from rising to the top."

They talked most of the morning. About careers and marriages and kids. About their dreams for the future. About life.

* * * * *

Chaplain (Lieutenant Colonel) Paul Eastley rang the door bell at the Andrews' family home and listened to the chimes he had activated resound within. They had been out of town the first time he called. He was leaving to go back on duty tomorrow. If they were not at home yet he feared he would miss them. Then he heard footsteps and the door opened to reveal Charlotte Andrews.

"Paul!" she exclaimed. "I was so sorry to hear about your mother. We would have attended the funeral had we been in town. Come in. Please come in. I'll go get Chalmers."

"Charlotte, it's nice to see you," he replied as he walked through the foyer and into the formal living room. Mrs. Andrews gestured to a large leather chair and he sat down there while she went to locate her husband. They returned together, she petite, brown-haired, with nice skin and dark eyes, he large and muscular for a man in his 60s. He and Paul hugged one another and he also expressed his regret at not having been able to attend the funeral of Edith Eastley.

"Well, Paul, at least the weather was better than it was when you came two years ago to bury Doug. That was one terrible storm." Both men were silent for a moment.

"How long have you been a lieutenant colonel, Paul?"

"Almost a year now, Chalmers. I got it in spite of some resistance in the Corps to giving it to me because of some things that happened in Viet Nam."

"Tell us more, Paul," Mrs. Andrews interjected.

"You probably know at least the outlines of it. Two purple hearts. The first when some kid drove alongside my jeep and flipped a grenade into it. I dove out the right side but it killed my driver." He touched the cicatrice of scars beside his right eye. "That's where I got these. Then there was the time I went on a search and destroy mission with my guys and we were ambushed. I helped get some of those wounded into Medevac choppers and on their way to a field hospital. I got shot. And, with all due respect, Mrs. Andrews, I won't show either of you where the scar from that is located." He smiled.

"And I was with Doug and his unit on an assault and we were all pinned down, outmanned and outgunned. Seemed like every time we tried to make a move, the enemy could bring fire to bear on us. Then I noticed a spotter with binoculars in a clump of trees. We had some tall grass, so I crept through that til I was just a few feet behind him, and then charged swinging my machete. Hit him on the back of the head with the flat of the blade. The Bible tells us that 'he who sheds blood, by man shall his blood be shed.' I avoided that." He chuckled. "In my case the guy just got a bruise and some swelling."

His listeners smiled appreciatively. "Thanks, Paul, for almost bringing us up to date. But what have you been doing since you came back from Viet Nam. I know you were at Fort Riley when you came up here to hold the funeral service for us."

45

"For a time I was assigned to the Chaplain School at Fort Hamilton in New York, actually on the tip of Brooklyn near the Verrazano Narrows Bridge. Then they sent me to Fort Leavenworth to attend the U.S. Army Command and General Staff College. I did so well in tactics that the school asked me to stay on for a time as a teacher. So I did. That may have helped override any objections to my being promoted that the Chaplain Corps had. So now here I am."

"Well," began Chalmers, "I pretty well decided after the funeral to semi-retire and do some traveling with Charlotte. As you know, we were pretty broken up by Doug's death. So we've gone on a number of cruises and road trips."

Charlotte added, "We've now been on six of the seven continents, and have a trip planned to see New Zealand and Australia soon. Then we will have seen them all. Traveling and seeing other people and places has helped, I think, a great deal, in letting us deal with the loss of our Doug." She grimaced.

"And when I'm home I still do a lot of work with our Get Rid of War group. It is the least I can do to honor his name."

Paul nodded. "I have been hearing a lot about GROW recently Charlotte. Good for you. I am proud of you. And how is Laura?"

"She's finishing college at the university this year. Planning on going into politics in one way or another. Sorry she isn't here to say 'hi,' but we will certainly tell her we had this opportunity to see you."

"Do you still hear from Nancy West?"

Chalmers answered. "She is the sweetest girl, so pretty, such a nice personality. An all-round nice person. She wrote us recently. She has a new friend. He has asked her to marry him and she has agreed. I hate this. I really hate this. I wanted that girl to be my daughter-in-law."

Charlotte made murmuring noises of agreement. "We don't know if she has set a date yet. She did say that when that day comes she hopes Chalmers and I will be able to attend. I don't know if we will. We would get all weepy-eyed and probably spoil what should be a memorable day for her."

"She is still in the Army Medical Service, working as a nurse at Brooke Army Hospital. All the people we love have been promoted. You. And she told us that she was now a major. She wrote that she was simply never going to get over the fact that Doug was gone forever. She would love him always, she said. But maybe she had grieved long enough. She needed a companion in life. Someday she wanted children. She told us his name is Jonathan Diedrich. He is a pharmaceutical salesman. They met at the hospital. She says he is a good man. She believes he will love her and treat her right. She says she doesn't love him—at least not in the way she loved Doug—but at least she likes him and feels comfortable with him. And maybe, she said, just maybe that will be enough."

"Oh Paul," Charlotte's eyes brimmed and then overflowed. "Life is not fair. Everything we ever wanted and hoped for and worked toward died with our son. I so wish I could have died in his place." She put her face in her hands and sobbed. She was sitting on a sofa beside her husband and Chalmers put his arms around her and pulled her close. She sniffled. She looked up at Paul, her tears now under control. "My!" she exclaimed. "I usually have more self-control than that."

They talked about Doug and his years growing up. Paul told of his friendship with Doug that had begun the day he marched his platoon to divine services in Viet Nam and had grown after that. He remembered being at Red Beach with Doug for R & R. He remembered how he had suffered when he learned that his platoon sergeant, Jan Szigmond, had died as a result of careless fire control within the platoon. He told of the long talks they had. He spoke of Doug's hatred of drugs. He recalled how sick Lieutenant Andrews had been before, with Paul's help, he was shipped off to the field hospital to recuperate. He related how energized Doug was when he returned to his unit and how enthusiastically he had been telling Paul about this girl—this nurse--he had met. He did his best to fill in Doug's father and mother with information about the last year of their son's life. They talked for hours. When they paused, Paul looked out through the large windows and saw that light had disappeared from the sky. It was late dusk. It was time to take his leave.

* * * * *

"Thank you for being patient with me, Jonathan. I appreciate it very much. I have thought and thought about the other night, and the beautiful ring, and the question you asked of me." Nancy West paused, her mind instantly remembering the idyll she and Doug had shared in Hawaii. She pressed on. If you want to marry me knowing that I am still sorrowing over the loss of Doug Andrews, then . . . then . . . then I will marry you."

* * * * *

CHAPTER FOUR

"Bless the Lord . . . who redeemeth thy life from destruction."–
Psalm CIII: 2a, 4a.

Ever since the day when Colonel Cao Ba Thien had tortured
him, Doug's control of his emotions had rarely been effective. The
pain that day had almost driven him out of his mind. Then there was
the shame he felt at having finally said the words demanded of him
by Thien. Add to that his skin fungus and the stomach parasites that
he knew lived once more in his gut, the spareness of his cell, the
lice, the cockroaches, the rats, the meager food, and the constant fear
that Colonel Thien would call him again for still more torture–all this
served to nearly unhinge Doug's mind. At one moment he might be
reasonably content, believing that some day this would all end and he
could go back to Nancy West. Without a moment's warning he could
fall into a slough of despond and a pit of despair. He often found
himself weeping, waking at night with tears on his cheeks, sitting at
noonday trying to stifle moans of painful memory.

Now suddenly the specter of his dead platoon sergeant, Jan
Szigmond, had materialized in his cell. Doug was filled with shock
and aweat seeing his beloved Polish sergeant and he began to weep,
his hands trembling uncontrollably. Huge racking sobs shook his
chest. "Jan? Jan? You are dead. Why are you here?"

"Be strong, Lieutenant. I am real. I am alive. Vill tell you
about it ven ve get the chance. Heard you vas here. You. Me. Ve
going to get out of dis place."

Andrews hugged the spare frame of Sergeant First Class Jan
Szigmond. "Jan, I don't know when I was ever so glad to see anyone
as I am to see you."

"Can't stay long, Lieutenant. Must keep on vith my vork or
guards get suspicious. I am trustee. Zey trust me and let me do liddle
things. I keep zem happy. Zey ask me to say tings, I say zem. Ask
me to write criticisms of U.S. I write zem. Vat they do to those who

resist is not good. No one belief such tings anyvay. Hear you vere hurt by lousy Colonel Thien. Ve repay him before ve leafe. Must go now. Vill be back. Eat everyzing in bowl. Put meat in. Vitamin pills too. Must make you strong."

And he was gone. But how was he here? He was dead, shot in the jungle by Terry, killed by the Viet Cong as he covered the retreat of his platoon.   Doug thought about possibilities as he wolfed down the rice and meat in his bowl. It seemed to be real beef and Andrews' mouth watered as he ate. He cleaned his bowl down to the last kernel of rice. Then he licked the bowl to make sure nothing remained. He held the vitamin pills given him by Szigmond in his hand and then dry-swallowed them.

* * * * *

It was almost as if Colonel Thien knew what had happened. He had not called for Andrews for weeks and now, an hour after Szigmond's visit, two guards entered Doug's cell, grabbed him and frogmarched him down to the interrogation room. Thien was waiting. He did not ask Andrews to sit in the empty chair poised in front of his desk. Doug stood at attention.

"It has been a long time, Captain."

"Yessir."

Thien gestured to a man standing nearby who had a motion picture camera trained on Doug.

"We need you to make some statements about your country's presence here and this man, *Ong* Chau, will film you saying them. Then we will release the film to western television."

He handed two sheets of paper to Doug.

"Look over this material. These are the things you will talk about."

Doug read them with sinking heart. He finished reading and, in a moment of defiance, crumpled them in his fist and dropped the wad of paper on the floor.

"Colonel, you know I can't say those things. They are not accurate. They are not true. I would be violating my oath as an officer to say those things in front of a camera."

Chau pulled the camera from the tripod, folded it, and quietly left the room.

"Oh, I think you will soon agree to say them, Captain."

Thien nodded to the two guards. They grabbed Doug and folded him onto the chair and tied him securely to it. Then one put a box in front of it and lifted Doug's legs so his feet lay squarely on top of the box. The guard adjusted the box so that Doug's feet now extended a few inches beyond the box. Terrified, Doug feared the unknown thing that was going to happen to him.

"One more chance, Captain. Will you say these things for the camera?"

Doug remembered learning through the tap code that Lieutenant Colonel Jerry Corley, the officer in command, had passed the word. Few men could long withstand the suffering that torture brought. Anyone could be broken. Yet they must resist. So Corley had decreed that, if possible, each man taken for interrogation must resist as long as he could, perhaps even to withstand initial torture, and only then was he free to cooperate with his captors. Such cooperation was, however, to be minimal and every effort was to be made to mix truth and lies, to mislead those who wanted information. It was rumored that one Navy flight officer, under questioning, finally admitted that the commander of the aircraft carrier on which he was based was named Clark Kent, information which his interrogator had solemnly recorded. The man was married to Lois Lane. His second in command was Billy Batson. All of this was accepted at face value by his solemn interrogators.

"Captain? What do you say?"

"Colonel, even if you hurt me I can't do what you ask. I am sorry. I have already apologized and asked forgiveness for what I did at Yen Song (3)."

The guards smirked at him. Then, with a nod from the colonel, one picked up a bamboo rod with its end split five ways. Without warning he swung the rod at the soles of Doug's feet. Pain blossomed all the way to the top of Doug's head. He screamed. Blood dripped from his feet onto the floor. The guard cocked his arm and swung again. And again. Again. The skin on Andrews' feet now hung in ribbons. Mercifully he slipped into unconsciousness.

Even that was not allowed. One guard brought a bucket of water into the room and dowsed Andrews with it. Spluttering, Doug roused. Again the other guard hit his feet.

"Oh god. Oh my god. Oh please stop. Please. Please. Please. Oh my god. Oh my Christ. Oh God, let me die."

Colonel Thien regarded him dispassionately. He nodded to the guard and held up three fingers. Three more times the guard swung at Doug's feet with all his might.

"Ahhhhhhh, Jesus. Ahhhhhh."

Again Doug passed out.

He knew nothing until later when he regained his senses and found he was back in his cell, lying on the floor next to his cot. The guards had brought him back and simply thrown him onto the hard concrete. He managed to climb slowly onto his cot.

His tongue lay thick in his mouth and his feet were in agony, but he managed to mutter a few words to himself. "By God, Thien, I am going to kill you. So help me God, I am going to kill you with my bare hands. Slowly. If it's the last thing I ever do, I am going to watch you die." Then he cried. His chest heaved as he strained against the agony in his feet. The pain was more than he could bear. His groans went on and on.

* * * * *

As if in a dream he saw Szigmond in his cell, bent over the cot, gently applying salve to his ruined feet. Doug cried out in pain as Szigmond ministered to his injuries. He felt himself lifted to a sitting position, a pill placed on his tongue, a cup of water held to his lips. He heard taps in the wall but was unable to understand what was being said. At morning and night his bowl contained real food. At first he was hardly able to swallow any of it, but as time passed, he was able to eat it with eagerness. He saw bandages on his feet. His body was bathed. He felt Szigmond periodically tenderly applying salve to them. He swallowed pain medications and vitamin pills. There came a day when he gingerly sat up and placed his feet on the floor and then

52

carefully stood up, wincing at their tenderness. But at least he was ambulatory again. Now if Colonel Thien would only let him alone long enough for him to regain his strength. Save for the knocking in the walls and the occasional momentary visit by Szigmond, he was left utterly alone in his cell. His only contact was with the guards and he prayed there would be no more confrontations with Colonel Thien.

Once again he began his exercise regimen. Push-ups. Sit-ups. Leg lifts. Pacing back and forth in his tiny cell, three steps one way, three steps back to his starting point. Lacking any kind of free weights or exercise machines, he learned how to pit one muscle against another, strengthening both in the process. Every day he exercised until he was exhausted, and then continued for another hour. Doug knew he looked terrible. His broken nose had healed badly. His hair was dirty, lank and long. He was unshaven, and had now grown a lengthy beard and mustache. His skin was full of rashes and he scratched his itches until he sometimes brought blood. Thin when he was shot, his capture and imprisonment had made Doug nearly skeletal. The flesh stretched tight over his skull, emphasizing his sunken eyes. When he looked down at his body he saw only toothpick arms and legs. Sometimes he smiled faintly at the thought that he would hardly be selected to serve as a poster boy during Army recruiting drives. But maybe the exercise and Szigmond's food and vitamins might help him regain some of his strength. That was his prayer.

Szigmond came and went. Each time he arrived he brought something to add to Doug's strength or to ease the pain in Doug's sore body. His feet still bled occasionally. His joints suffered from an arthritic-like pain from having been dislocated on the pulley during the first incident of torture ordered by Colonel Thien. His broken ribs still bothered but were slowly mending.

They talked. Not all at one time, but over a period of days and weeks, Doug told Szigmond all that had happened since they had last seen one another. Doug told how he had punished Specialist Terry, indeed had almost killed him, for his panicked shot which had wounded Jan. He told how he was no longer a lieutenant but a captain, how he had been given his own company in the battalion commanded by Lieutenant Colonel Jeremiah Barrett. He told about Szigmond's successor, First Sergeant Harold Spruance. He told of the assault on Yen Song (3) ordered by the brigade commander, Colonel Vernon "Savage" Moore. He told how Lieutenant Norman Crosse had died from a booby trap explosion, how rifle fire from the village had killed Staff Sergeant Leroy Johnson and George Catlett. With words torn from his very soul, he described to Szigmond the events that followed, the destruction of Yen Song (3), and his own part therein. His eyes became fixed upon some distant spot only he could see, a thousand yard stare, as he remembered those hours at Yen Song (3). He recollected for Szigmond how the Viet Cong 48th Local Force Battalion had materialized out of thin air to hunt down and kill every last member of the platoon that had visited death upon Yen Song (3) and how the battalion *chieu hoi*, Le Qui Thanh, had shot him in the chest. He told of riding in the pickup, of his stay at the primitive Viet Cong field hospital in the jungle, of his transfer to this place.

Captain Andrews also told Platoon Sergeant Jan Szigmond about meeting Nancy West, about how they had fallen in love, how he had given her an engagement ring, how they planned to marry upon his return from Viet Nam. That DEROS date was now months upon months in the past. He was not even sure how long it had been. He shared with Szigmond how his thoughts were often consumed by memories of her. He told how he worried about her, that she would be alright during this enforced separation. He was concerned that she was worried over what had become of him. Army Graves Registration would be able to find bodies for the rest of the platoon, but they would not locate a corpse for Captain Douglas MacArthur Andrews. Doug knew he was now probably listed as a POW, presumed KIA. How would Nancy react to such news? How would his parents and sister feel? Would they believe that, somewhere, somehow, he was still alive? Or would they believe he was dead, one of those unidentifiable corpses that so often litter a battlefield?

To all this Jan Szigmond listened sympathetically, patiently. In short bursts he also told Doug how he came to be in the prison. He and

Post and Johnson had already taken out the two roving 3-man patrols that circled the perimeter of the jungle bunker. He had been poised to throw his Randall knife at the lone guard manning a listening post on the top of the bunker. He grimaced as he remembered how the blast from Terry's accidental and nervous pulling of the trigger on his M-16 had picked him up and then thrown him to the ground, shot in the back, the bullet passing on through his chest without striking lung or heart, but disabling his arm. He got up only to be shot by the Viet Cong, through the leg, his femur shattered. *"Phicrova,"* he cursed as he fell. "Red Man" Finch had pulled him back to temporary safety. Already there were other casualties in the platoon caused by enemy fire. *"Holiara"* Szigmond swore.

"Red Man" told how they would rig a stretcher to use to carry the sergeant back to their own lines. At his orders, they left without him, while with an M-16 and an M-60 he lay on the jungled ground of Viet Nam and held off the Viet Cong who wanted to kill his men. Then he passed out from loss of blood.

Sometime later he wakened to find himself still lying on the jungle floor with an enemy soldier guarding him with a rifle. A Viet Cong medic worked on him, staunching the flow of blood and splinting his leg. When he finished, soldiers pulled Szigmond to a nearby vehicle and threw him in. As had happened to Andrews, so also did it happen to Szigmond. He was treated initially in a Viet Cong field hospital, this one dug out below the surface of the ground, large enough to care for up to twenty wounded at a time. He recuperated there from his chest wound. Eventually as that got better he regained use of his arm.

His leg remained in splints for three months. Finally it healed to the point where he could stump around and he made the most of his recuperation. He had learned some Vietnamese when he had fought in French Indochina with the Foreign Legion in the late 1940s and the first half of the following decade. Later he had added to his vocabulary when he returned to Asia as a member of the U.S. Army. Because of this smattering of their tonal language, his captors talked to him rather than ignoring him. They allowed him limited freedom of movement.

Then came the day when he was transferred to the prison in which he and Doug now sat talking. He also had met Colonel Cao Ba Thien. Shortly after his arrival he had been taken to the interrogation room. There he met Thien. As had happened with Doug, Thien told Szigmond that he would have to apologize to the Vietnamese people and to make certain statements to the world press on behalf of the war the Democratic Republic of Viet Nam was fighting with the Republic of Viet Nam and with the United States.

Jan was an old pro. He knew nothing of a military nature that would be beneficial to the North Vietnamese. He also believed it would do no harm to apologize to them for the air and ground wars that had raged for many years, killing villagers by the hundreds, bombs falling on targets that could not conceivably be thought of as strategic or tactical sites. He was, lastly, not at all opposed to making a film in which he might ask the United States to stop doing those things that killed such villagers.

So when Thien confronted him, Szigmond snapped to attention and called out "Yessir," as if he stood on a parade ground. The colonel stared at him open-mouthed. At last he had found a willing prisoner. And so, following his perfunctory apology and a film in which he said nothing of importance, Sergeant First Class Jan Szigmond became a prison trustee. Not once had he been subjected to the tender mercies of the torturing Colonel Thien. As months passed and Jan continued to be cooperative in everything asked of him, he was allowed more and more liberty. His cell door usually remained unlocked so he could come and go at will. His cell was cleaner, his mattress thicker, his blanket softer. He was never left in chains as were other, more recalcitrant prisoners. His food ration was better. He could go outside into the courtyard when the mood struck him. Other prisoners used him as a go-between to carry messages. He often took information from Lieutenant Colonel Jerry Corley, the American officer in charge here among the POWs to one or another of the imprisoned inmates. And he could plan.

He planned well. Jan knew that one day he would attempt an escape from this hell hole and he wanted to be prepared. So he began to amass supplies that might help him achieve his freedom and a return to American lines. He manufactured a knife patterned on the Randall knife he had once worn, making it from a scrap of steel he found in one of the storage rooms of the prison. A length of wire, with loops made at each end, became a *garote*. To his growing store of weapons he added a coil of rope. One never knew when a stretch of rope might come in handy. He made a wooden baton. He made *ninja* throwing stars. He found and repaired a broken machete, sharpening it until it cut like a razor. He stole a guard's pistol and from another confiscated a supply of ammunition. He had the pleasure of listening to the tortured screams of both men as they were punished for their carelessness. He located canned food and added it to his private stores. He stole medical supplies and laid them aside for some future emergency. He located and stole backpacks and canteens and food tins. From the kitchen he got a twenty-five pound bag of rice to use as emergency rations. He put aside dried instant coffee packets. He found concentrated chocolate bars and, resisting the temptation to gorge on them, put them away for the future. He put aside a large stock of vitamins and a supply of chlorine tablets for purifying water so it could be drunk. He was proud of his treasure and kept it under lock and key in a forgotten shack at the rear of the prison. And he did all this under the very noses and watchful eyes of the prison guards.

He had always intended to leave this vicious place where the screams of tortured men punctuated both the days and the nights. If he could have done so, he would have headed a breakout of all the POWs housed here. That was not possible. Now, however, fate had placed in his care one of the few men he had ever fully respected. He would take Captain Douglas MacArthur Andrews with him when he left. And they would leave over the dead body of Colonel Thien.

During their talks, Doug asked Jan if he knew where they were. He admitted to having become totally disoriented during the first weeks and months of his captivity until now he was even unsure which way was north and he had no idea at all how far south American lines lay. Jan informed him that he had stored away a map he had 'requisitioned' from an unwary guard. He said he did not need to

57

consult it to know their approximate location. They were in Quang Binh province, in An Nam.

Doug knew that Viet Nam had historically been divided into three parts. The southern area, governed by the Republic of Viet Nam, was Cochin China. The north, controlled by the Democratic Republic of Viet Nam, had for a thousand years been the most important part of the nation and historically the first to have been settled. It was Ton Kin and the capital city was Ha Noi. The long thin portion that connected the two was An Nam, in recent history the place where the Vietnamese emperor lived in his Citadel in the city of Hue. The line dividing north and south ran through the middle of An Nam along the 17th parallel, not far north of the emperor's home city.

* * * * *

It seemed that Doug could never escape the land of nightmares where all action was either killing or being killed. There were no rules. There were enemies everywhere. The strain brought on by watchfulness, by waiting, by listening for death's siren song wore him down. Once again Doug, wearing full combat gear, strode toward Yen Song (3). He and his platoon stormed the little hamlet, firing into hooches, and engaging in an orgy of killing unarmed boys and girls, violating young women, slaughtering the elderly. Was that him in the lead? Or someone else? Had he actually been at Yen Song (3) or were these thoughts simply an illusion based on the experiences of others and his own year in-country? Maybe the whole thing had never really happened. He was, after all, a decent person, the son of Chalmers and Charlotte Andrews, one of the most prominent families in Nebraska. He had no bad intentions. What had happened at Yen Song (3) was certainly not intentional on his part. It arose on the spur of the moment, when the minds of the American soldiers were still in shock at the sudden death of three of their number. Doug had not wanted any of it to happen. It just had!

He pretended that it was all simple imagination. Since he didn't want to have done it, and couldn't have done it because he was not that kind of soldier, it simply hadn't happened at all. And even if it had happened, was it actually so damning? Collateral damage.

58

The intentional or accidental killing of civilian noncombatants in a war zone. In Viet Nam there was no pacified zone separate from the war zone. The whole nation had been designated a war zone by the American high command. Noncombatants? Who could tell? Rumors told how whores secreted razor blades in their vaginas to punish sex-driven American soldiers. Old women and young smuggled arms and ammunition in those baskets hanging from their shoulder poles. Young boys threw hand grenades into buses transporting soldiers through the streets of Sai Gon. 'Innocent' farmers of the south planted booby traps along American troop walkways in order to kill a few and frighten those who survived. That, after all, was how Second Lieutenant Norman Crosse had died.

Collateral damage? Who were the noncombatants who should be left alone in this war-ruined country? The people of Yen Song (3) had undoubtedly given their young men into the service of the Viet Cong. They gave of their rice harvest to help feed their sons and the sons of others who fought against the Americans and the Army of Viet Nam, the military force of the southern government. There could be little doubt that the inhabitants of Yen Song (3) carried information between units of the Viet Cong. In what sense, then, were they noncombatants? So what did it matter if they had been slaughtered? They knew the risks when they chose allegiance to the Viet Cong.

Military units of ARVN were known to have slaughtered entire villages suspected of 'traitorous' activities. The soldiers of South Korea who fought as allies of America in Viet Nam belonged either to the Tiger Division or to the White Horse Division. When they moved into an area, they killed at will to inspire caution and fear among the inhabitants. Wherever they moved, heads of local people came to decorate poles jammed strategically into the earth, and those soldiers suffered few casualties. The Viet Cong simply left them alone.

In such contexts was the massacre at Yen Song (3) so bad? Doug dreamed on, his sleep troubled. If he could forget what had happened, if he could finally tell himself it was all his imagination, then one day when he returned to Nancy and his family he could put

59

it all behind him and go on with his life for Yen Song (3) had actually never happened.

Most soldiers, Doug dreamed, are righteous, God-fearing boys when they are pulled into the Green Machine. The draft has poked its way into every corner of America to find these young men. Then they spent eight weeks in basic training and a further eight weeks in advanced individual training. They are shown how to do horrible things. Their tutelage by the Army informed them that, at certain times, they must act inhumanely if they are to succeed at the tasks to which they have been ordered. Where was the line drawn between acceptable inhumanity and savagery? Was Yen Song (3) a war crime? Or an accident? Or an allowable incident occurring within the fog of war? Who would decide?

Was Yen Song (3) murder? A massacre? Or simply a mission ordered by legitimate authority that went horribly wrong? Decisions made while under fire, as he had been, are often not good ones. So he was innocent of any war crimes. But if he was so innocent, then why did he suffer such personal anguish? Many years later, a prominent American, once a team leader of a SEAL unit, would refer to his own dilemma with the words: "We received fire. We returned fire. But when the firing stopped, we had killed only women, children, and older men. It was not a military victory. It was a tragedy, and I had allowed it." That was precisely Doug's dilemma. He had allowed a ferocious barrage of automatic rifle fire and grenades. Blood and torn animal and human guts lay splattered throughout the torched and fire-blackened community. If those in the hamlet who died were not innocent, at least they were not guilty. An accidental atrocity. In war, innocent people get killed. That is the way it has been ever since Cain slew Abel. And so Doug dreamed his nightmares and his mind, ever wakeful, tried to sort out what had happened and find some way to exonerate himself.

* * * * *

"Ze line dividing norrth and south rruns along ze 17th parallel, not farr from the emperror's city of Hue," Szigmond said. "But you know zat, Captain. Vot you don't know is how farr norrth ve arre. I tell you." He unfolded the precious map he had stolen. "Ve are right here, Captain, in Quang Binh province in An Nam. See? Province of Quang Binh, canton of Dai Phong, , district of Le Thuy, sub district of Quang Ninh. That's pretty definite, Captain, discovered in talks with guards. Nearest town is An Xa. Most people poor peasants, renting land zey farrm. Grow mainly rice and sweet potatoes. Three nearrby rivers. Ze Gianh. Ze Nhat Le. Ze Kien Giang. Nearby two large lakes. Lake Bau Tro, located rright herre. Guards say zat lake has shape of Chinese ink pot. Ze otherr lake is Hac Hai, about one and half miles across. Good fishing. Many people get much food from fishing. Around lake special watermelon grow as produce to export to country. Jungle nearby. Mountains of Annamese Cordillera to west. South China Sea to east. Biggest towns are Dong Hoi and Vinh. Big military base at Vinh. Coastal navy of north goverrnment based zere." Szigmond carefully refolded the map and replaced it inside his shirt.

"If ve know ze lay of ze land, Captain, ve can escape zis place! Big problem is making our escape and zen going 320 kilometers south to ze 17th parallel!"

Doug nodded solemnly and swore in his heart not only that they would escape but that he would punish the colonel who had hurt him so badly and the guards who had treated him so brutally.

* * * * *

It was almost as if Colonel Thien could listen to their conversations. Could he somehow know that they planned to escape? That very evening guards came for Doug and frogmarched him to the interrogation room.

"Good evening, Captain," said Colonel Thien, seated behind his table. "I see that your feet have healed very well. You are again able to walk and stand on them. I congratulate you on your healing powers." His black eyes bored into Doug's. "It is almost as if you have had someone to help you heal your feet. . . . No matter. You are here with me again, now. Have you yet come to your senses? Are you now willing to make a film for us?

Doug shuddered. He knew what his answer had to be. He also knew that the colonel planned some new torment for him if he did not cooperate.

"Sir, my rank is captain. My name is Douglas MacArthur Andrews. My service number is . . . "

Thien waved him to silence. Then, in a conversational tone, he said "have you ever read books about your namesake? I have. MacArthur was great general. He took good care of his men. He saw to it that as few as possible paid the supreme price for conquering Hapon. You would say Japan. He was brave. He was a genius at planning battles." Then he paused. "Are you as brave as he, Captain?"

Thien got up from his seat behind the table and began to walk toward his private door out of the room. Then he hesitated, turned around, and spoke to his guards. "Put him in irons."

The guards pushed and shoved Andrews out of the room and down the corridors to his cell. As they neared it, they passed Jan Szigmond busily sweeping the corridor. He did not look up as they passed, but his presence there gave Doug momentary hope.

It did not last long. While one guard remained with him in his cell, the other vanished down the hall. He shortly returned carrying manacles that dated back to the days of French colonization of Indochina. Two straight bars. Four horseshoe shaped bars, the ends of each fitting within four holes in each straight bar. The guards took Andrews to the floor. He lay there supine, not struggling, wondering what was going to happen.

Working quickly, one guard fastened horseshoe bars in place, one over each of Doug's wrists, fit their ends into the straight bar, and, with a wrench, began to tighten the nuts that fit on the exposed ends of the U-bar bolts. The other guard did the same to his ankles. They smiled as they worked. They enjoyed their job.

"This isn't so bad," Doug thought. "It will just mean I won't have any mobility until they come back and take them off." Then he noticed that the leg irons and handcuffs, already tight, were bringing ever more pressure to bear on his wrists and ankles. The guards continued to tighten the nuts. Now they resorted to using a wrench to tighten them still more. The metal bit into Doug's flesh, more harshly with every passing second.

Now the pain began, but still the guards continued their work, talking to one another and laughing as they gripped their wrenches. Ever tighter. The pain was now severe. Doug writhed, but he was helpless. There was nothing he could do except to watch the guards fastening the irons on him. When the guards were finally satisfied, the U-bars and the straight bars had been made so tight that they not only cut into his flesh cruelly, but actually sat on bone. No circulation of blood was now able to get past the dams they created on his body. His hands and feet reddened, pulsated, and then began to swell.

Their work finished, the guards left the cell. Andrews still lay on the floor. He hardly noticed the cold stone under his body. His consciousness focused solely on the increasingly intense pain in his ankles and wrists. He called out for help, but no one came. Where, he wondered, was Szigmond? Szigmond ought to be able to do something to help him. As the pain worsened, Doug began screaming. He could not bend far enough to see his feet but when he looked at his hands he saw that they had swollen to the size of cantaloupes and were now turning black. Was this how it was all going to end? A quadruple amputee no longer able to hold anything nor to stand or walk? Certainly no longer able to walk the two hundred miles south to American lines. His shrill screams bounced off the scabrous walls of his cell.

Someone kicked him in the ribs. He opened his eyes as he sobbed and saw that, for the first time, Colonel Thien had come to visit him in his cell. "What do you think, Captain? Will Nebraska Wesleyan be able to beat Doane College in football this year? I miss having regular news of Nebraska sports. You probably follow them regularly. I still remember the school's football schedule. The team played the University of Sioux Falls, Concordia University in Seward, Hastings College, Northwestern College in Orange, Iowa, Dana College in Blair, Midland Lutheran College in Fremont, Briar Cliff and Morningside Colleges in Sioux City, Doane College and Dakota Wesleyan. I have a good memory, do I not? I used to go to every

63

home game and to as many away games as I could manage. It was fun. Did you ever play football yourself?"

Doug's chest heaved as he tried to stifle his cries of pain.

"My rank is Captain. My name is Douglas MacArthur Andrews . . . and fuck you Colonel!"

"I personally believe that Doane will probably prevail. Well, in any case, let someone know when you are ready to be the star of your own film. Just call for a guard. One will be outside, close enough to hear you. Don't wait too long. I want you to still have the ability to walk and to use your hands."

For some hours after Thien left, Doug was tormented by the pain the irons caused him. Then, miraculously, the pain eased. While surcease from torment was wonderful, a glance at his hands caused him to cry out in dismay. They were now very black. They were hugely swollen, so large that in places the skin had split open. And they had absolutely no feeling. Doug knew that he and Szigmond were never going to escape this place. He was going to die here.

* * * * *

Twenty-four hours passed. Then thirty. Doug hallucinated, and once again, as so many times before, he walked the streets of Yen Song (3), firing his weapon at fleeing villagers. Then he was with Nancy West, explaining to her why it had been necessary to kill those people. "I had to, Nancy. Colonel Thien was somewhere in the village, hiding, and I had sworn I was going to kill him. But no matter how many died, I never found him. He got away!"

He roused, still thinking of Nancy. He tried to remember every detail of every hour they had spent together. What she had worn. What color her lipstick was. What they ordered to eat at the restaurants on Waikiki Beach. How ardent she was. He thought of the letters they had exchanged, of the promises they had made, of the life they sought to have. His thoughts skittered away into darkness.

Someone knelt beside him. He opened his eyes. The two guards were back with their wrenches. Were they going to tighten the nuts even more? Doug cried out helplessly. He watched them as they fitted their wrenches on the nuts. And then–the Lord be praised–

Andrews discovered what they were doing. They were loosening the nuts, freeing the U-bolts so they could be withdrawn from the straight bars. Then they were off. The guards picked up the irons and their wrenches and left the cell, carefully locking the door behind them.

Doug managed to get on his knees and elbows and make his way onto the cot. He lay there panting, grateful that the pressure had been taken away from his wrists and ankles. He looked at them. They were huge–and totally useless, unable to move and without feeling. Even as he watched, some of the blackness began to fade away. The recirculating blood was now free to penetrate again into his hands and feet. As it carried away accumulated poisons and brought tissue-saving blood to his extremities, the torment grew and grew until he howled. It hurt like a bitch. He gagged from the pain. This was a nightmare that seemed as if it was never going away. Hours passed before the swelling began to go down, before the blood-starved tissues stopped demanding oxygen rich blood, before the pain began to lessen.

Still his hands and feet were useless. He experimented, trying to pick up his food bowl from the floor only to find that it slipped through nerveless fingers and rolled away across the floor. He tried to stand, but it felt as if no feet were attached to his ankles. He sobbed and lay back on his bunk. Two days passed before he was able to use them at all, and even then they moved in unreliable ways. Doug swore that he would survive, if for no other reason than to kill Colonel Thien who had made him suffer so endlessly. In all that time, except for the brief glimpse in the corridor, he had not seen Sergeant Szigmond.

On the third day following Doug's release from the irons, he heard a furtive sound of a key turning the lock on his cell and Szigmond slipped in. Doug was lying on his cot, still suffering from the brutal irons. Szigmond lifted Andrews to a sitting position and put a water flask to his lips.

"Drink, Captain. You are dehydrated."

Doug greedily sucked the water. Szigmond   pulled the flask away.

"Slowly, Captain Andrews. Not too much at a time."

Held erect by Szigmond, Doug began to sob. The first ones degenerated into desperate, angry sobs of hurt and pain.

"Jan," he said, "I don't want . . . I am not going to *let* them hurt me again. I will kill myself before I go through another time like the last few days. Let's get out of here while I still can. But on the way out I am going to kill that son of a bitch."

Both men knew which son of a bitch Doug referred to. His sobs slowly subsided. The pain and agony he had suffered since his capture had utterly destroyed his ability to control his emotions, and an occasional sob continued to escape his chest. Jan continued to put the flask to his mouth. After Doug had drunk his fill, Jan handed him a small cloth bag in which Andrews found bread, meat of some kind, and a ball of sticky rice. He ate as if famished. In truth, he was!

"I voud have come soonerr, Captain," Szigmond whispered, "but zey had guard in ze hall most of ze time. Nossing I could do."

Doug nodded.

Jan then handed Doug a tennis ball.

"Here, Captain. Squeeze zis all ze time until hands worrk rright again. Walk back and forth til feet seem o.k. Then ve go. No more will you be tortured. No reason to stay longer. We find ourr way back home. First, beforre ve leave, some 'tings to do herre. So zey will remember us. Our escape will be forr zem a time to rremember."

Doug was still too sore and frail to be enthusiastic but he nodded his head and gave Szigmond a grim smile. He stood and extended his hand so they could clasp in oath to one another. When Szigmond gripped his hand, Doug had to smother a groan. His damn hands were still nearly useless.

"How often do guys here die?" he asked Jan.

Szigmond shook his head. "Too many. Perhaps one a veek or two a month. Big unmarked cemetery on grounds herre. At least two men won't end up therre!"

* * * * *

When Doug thought about how his life was slipping away from him, he shook his head in dismay. He had arrived in Viet Nam on 1 March 1966. He should have flown home on a "freedom bird" about 1

March 1967. Ten days before his DEROS had been the assault on Yen Song (3). He was wounded, captured, became a prisoner. It had been four months before his chest wound had healed at all. Then weeks of interrogation by Le Hong Lam, lasting perhaps two months. Next came the transfer to the horror house that now imprisoned him and the weeks and months of incarceration and torture. He couldn't be sure, and Szigmond was no help on this point, but Doug believed he had been here for about a year. It was now sometime in late-1968 or early 1969.. A lot of time had passed since he had walked the killing fields of Yen Song (3).

Several days passed quietly during which Szigmond did not visit him. Doug spent the hours in exercises in an attempt to give his withered muscles some tone again. He paced. He squeezed his tennis ball. He pitted sets of muscles against others. He did sit-ups and push-ups and leg lifts. He worked on these things until he felt light headed. He was not at all sure they were doing him any good, but neither were they harming him. He wanted every advantage possible when the time came to escape.

Remembering how much Jan had encouraged and helped him, he spent time during his exercises trying to remember as much as he could about the background of his platoon sergeant. He recalled how men in his unit altered Jan's Polish name into "Sick Man," for, they said, anyone who messed with him in or out of combat was sure to end up a very sick man.

* * * * *

Born in Grodzisk Mazowiecki, near Pruszko, southeast of Warszawa, eight year old Jan Szigmond saw invading German armies devastate his country in 1939. When he was barely into his teens he served as a volunteer runner for a Polish underground cell after his parents were arrested by the Nazis and sent to Auswiecim. People in the West would later come to know it by its German name: Auschwitz. Jan never saw them again. In 1944 and 1945, during the Soviet advance through Poland toward Berlin, Captain Ivan Petrovski of the 405th People's Tank Regiment allowed a husky young Pole to attach himself to his unit. No one questioned Jan as to his age; perhaps no one cared. By April 1945, as Berlin burned, fourteen year old Jan had become a killer of Germans.

Cast adrift among the sea of rootless humans moving across Europe at war's end, young Szigmond stayed for a time in a displaced persons camp in France. There he met a recruiter for *La Legion Etrangere des Francaises*, the French Foreign Legion, and directly Jan found a new purpose in life. It was as a Legionnaire that he received his first formal military training despite the fact that he was already a skilled soldier. He served in North Africa fighting Tuaregs until 1952 when he was transferred to Indochina to fight Viet Minh soldiers. When his enlistment expired, he migrated to the United States.

In 1959, as an alien, he enlisted in the U.S. Army. He had taught himself to speak fluent English but was never able to rid himself of his Slavic accent. Once again, as with the Legion, he found himself a private soldier. To his indignation he again had to go through a basic training course. He then completed airborne training. Assigned to a unit, he was rapidly promoted and in mid-1960 he transferred to the fledgling Army Special Forces.

By late 1963, aged thirty-two, Sergeant Szigmond was again in Southeast Asia, this time assigned as an adviser to a Vietnamese army unit. After a year in Indochina he was wounded and sent back to the States. Stateside duty bored him so in mid-1965 he put in a request for overseas reassignment and for the third time in his life found himself in Indochina, a member of Alpha Company, Second Battalion, 11th Brigade (Separate), 23rd Infantry Division where, after a year, he was promoted to Sergeant First Class.

When it came time for his estimated return from overseas duty, or DEROS, he voluntarily extended his time six months. Then a second extension. Then a third. He told acquaintances–no one was sure whether he had ever had a real friend-- that when the time came, he would extend still again. He had no desire for stateside duty. It was while a member of Alpha Company that he came into contact with a recently arrived second lieutenant named Douglas MacArthur Andrews. Wary of him at first, Szigmond slowly developed a fondness for the young officer and decided to train him in ways to stay alive in combat.Now both he and Doug were imprisoned in this hell hole. There had to be a way out. All it would take was careful planning.

* * * * *

"Big building," Jan said to Doug as in a midnight hour they sat on his bunk trying to figure out the best way to escape. "Have idea. Colonel Thien lives here. Almost neverr leaves building. Has aparrtment on second floor. He wears a pistol, but has no other weapons. He neverr comes to firrst floor at night to check on prisoners. He not really verry smart. He assigns only fourr guards to patrol here on first floor during night hours. They vulnerrable."

He held up his master key to the compound. "At night, everyzing is quiet. I let self out of cell. I open outside door and go to storrage shed. Pick up pistol. Come back in. Also have knife," referring to the imitation Randall he had made from scrap steel. "Once in again, I slip up on guards. Slit throats. If can't kill with knife, kill vith pistol. But don't vant to. If fire pistol, make alarm to guards in outside barracks. If zey come, too many to fight. Zen zey kill us. Also need it quiet so as to surprise Thien. Zen get you out of cell. Ve go upstairs to Colonel Thien's apartment. Break in. Find him. Kill him."

"Zen back down to firrst florre. Open all cell doors. Tell everyone is free to go if want. Some will do so. Others not. Too weak. Too wounded. Too afraid. Big breakout. Everybody get chance to spit on bodies of guards and Colonel Thien. Zen all others outfit selves with whatever find inside prison. Food. Weapons. Clothing. Whatever. You, me, ve stick together. Ve follow map. Ve carry packs. Ve have good canteens. Ve be o.k."

"It's a good plan, Jan. Let's do it."

"Tomorrow night no moon. Two, maybe three nights when otherrs find it hard to see or hunt us. Ve go then. O.K.? Tomorrow night. Be rready." He slipped from the cell quietly shutting the door behind him. Doug heard the key grate in the lock. All was still.

* * * * *

Twelve hours to wait. Time seemed to refuse to turn the hours. Doug spent most of that time trying to recall what his military mentors had tried to teach him. Lessons learned in ROTC and Ranger School

69

had been underscored by Sergeant Szigmond shortly after he arrived in Viet Nam. "Be careful when you're moving. Hurry can kill you. Be careful crrossing open terrain. If it's open, look for tracks. Always look for places where enemy might be hiding. Watch birds. If zey fly quickly from trees, be cautious. When moving thru jungle watch the way vines hang. If zey haf been moved, their leaves vill be twisted, zer tails pulled loose. Watch for machete hacks in elephant grass. Ven thirsty don't run up to first stream and dive in. Vait. Vatch. Apprroach cautiously. At night walk like Wietnamese. Hard for zem to see you, so maybe not be alarmed. Avoid easy way if possible. Enemies watch easy ways and set traps. Manchurian Rakes. Deadfalls. Punji stake pit. Ambush. Behind everry bush, up everry tree, in every clump of yungle grass, zere may be waiting enemy, and not all of them vill be human. There is notting easy about zis, but zere is notting mysterious either."

For a time Andrews remembered things he had been taught and then turned his mind to what he had learned on his own once given command of a platoon in Viet Nam. It did not work. Instead of recalling his escape from Nui Vu or the vanishing VC and the underwater cave at Tra Bong, or stand down at Red Beach, or the VC ambush that ruined Ensenlaube's knee, or any of the other moments of combat and terror that had filled his life for nearly a year, he saw only the burning wreckage of Yen Song (3).

This time his imagination showed him a different picture. As if he were there, he saw that a day had passed. Acrid smoke still rose from the fires of yesterday. A single starving dog slunk through the settlement, feeding on the corpses lying everywhere. Ducks and geese still swam in the village pond and nearby chickens pecked the earth looking for delicacies. A water buffalo with a wound in its side stood with trembling legs, blowing its pain through mucous filled nostrils. Inhabitants of nearby hamlets wandered slowly and purposefully through the desolation of Yen Song (3) come to bury the bodies of the slain. Already they had begun to bloat, to rupture, to smell. Those who came wore masks over their mouths and noses. The neighbors struggled to lift bodies and to carry them to an assembly area where they were laid out in rows, one after another after another.

The workers muttered in their tonal language when among the bodies they found three pregnant women. Bodies of infants and the very young were handled with particular respect. Girls and women who had been stripped and raped were covered with cloth. In the remnants of one hut they found the bodies of the hamlet elder, his sixty-four year old wife, and the couple's four grandchildren, ranging in age from one to fourteen. In one area some fifteen or sixteen corpses were piled on top of one another, probably shot with the platoon's M-60 machine gun.

Those who worked with the dead sometimes found relatives: a sister or sister-in-law, nieces and nephews, an uncle. They continued their sad task. A shallow mass grave was dug. Corpses were prepared and lowered into it. Funeral fires were lit. Solemn people from nearby hamlets came to talk and to pay their respects. A wail of mourning rose. Doug found himself standing beside two elderly people who were sorrowing at the community's loss. "I didn't mean to do it," he said over and again. "I didn't mean it."

* * * * *

Andrews came awake with a start as Szigmond slipped into his cell. As he stood to greet his friend his clothes looked like rags on a scarecrow, and he absent-mindedly scratched at the ever present itches on his body. Szigmond wore a look of excitement on his usually dour and immobile face. In with him he dragged a terrified guard, one of those who had tortured Doug to the very edge of the abyss that lies beyond sanity. Holding the guard with one hand, a blood-drenched Szigmond carried his bloody Randall knife in the other.

"Four guards," he enunciated. "Yust as I thought there would be. Now only one. Thought you might like to talk to him." With a gentle under- handed throw, the Sergeant tossed his knife to Andrews who carefully caught it by its wet and claret-red handle. The guard's eyes bugged and terror filled his face. "*Khong. Khong.*" he screeched. "No. No." Without a moment's hesitation, a look of determination on his face, Andrews stepped up to the guard and in two savage motions sliced the carotids on both sides of his neck. He followed with a stab to the man's lower belly and an upward slicing motion that carried the knife up to the guard's sternum. The man's greasy gut began spilling out onto the floor as, still not realizing he was dead, the guard again tried to call for help. On the floor of the cell he flopped spasmodically. Andrews kicked him harshly in the side and spoke to dead ears. "There, you son of a bitch! How do you like it when someone hurts you?" He wiped his bloody hands on his trousers and handed the blade back to Szigmond.

They moved into the corridor where a near-armory awaited them. The sergeant had collected the weaponry of all four guards. Four AK-47s. Four 9mm pistols. It was an unexpected windfall. Doug and Szigmond each grabbed a rifle and a pistol.

"Let's find Colonel Thien," Doug muttered. He had been to that part of the prison often enough. He knew which corridor to take and when to move into another. They came to the door of the interrogation room and carefully eased it open. Silence. They moved quietly through the large room with its torture equipment and over to the door that must lead to Colonel Thien's quarters.

"No shots fired yet," Szigmond said. "Didn't have to. So Thien may not know ve have taken over."

In turn he received a grim nod as Andrews placed his hand on the knob and slowly opened the door. It moved on well-oiled hinges. They entered and found themselves in a living area. Off to one side was a small kitchen redolent of rice and spices. Another door to the left. They crept up to it and carefully swung it open. There inside they could see a bed holding a sleeping form.

Doug stood beside the bed looking down upon this hated man. He decided on the best way to awaken him and so took the muzzle of the AK-47 and pushed it against one of Thien's eyes. An eye punch. No man could fake sleep or death when his eye had been hurt like that. Thien awoke with a startled cry and sat up holding his injured eye.

"You!" he said to Doug and, turning to the other man standing over him, he added "And you! How dare you people be in here. I will have you both tortured to death. The last sound you make will be a scream for mercy."

Szigmond reversed his AK-47 and used the butt to club Thien in the head. He and Andrews grabbed Thien from his bed and held him between them. Now they would begin what they had so often discussed and dreamed about. They would witness the demise of this monster.

They dragged him into the interrogation room and dropped Thien face down on the floor. While Doug knelt on his back and held his arms, Szigmond picked up some nearby short lengths of rope and tied Thien's hands securely. Then he began looping rope higher and higher til he reached the elbows. Doug grabbed the rope and pulled with all his might. The colonel's elbows inched closer to one another. More rope. More pulling. Finally the shoulders of the Vietnamese parted and his arms came together from wrist to shoulder. What he had ordered for so many others now came to be his lot in life.

They sat Thien on a chair while rigging another rope through the overhead pulley. Doug turned to his prisoner and snarled, "Why aren't you talking about the damned Nebraska Wesleyan football team now? You think about it so often. Why not now?"

Thien groaned. "You don't have to do this, Captain. Leave this apartment, go back to your cells, and I will insure that your treatment improves and that you are repatriated to your own lines."

"Do they still play Crete or Hastings College?" Doug asked as he fastened one end of the rope to Thien's wrists while the other end was threaded around the pulley and hung down toward the floor.

Then, with both Szigmond and Andrews pulling, they began to lift Thien from the floor by his wrists and dislocated shoulders. When they had gotten him a few feet into the air they stopped and affixed a ten pound weight to each ankle. Then they resumed pulling him higher. Higher. The ceiling was twenty feet high. The rope pulling Thien was almost through the pulley. He was nearly to the ceiling. Then the two men released the rope and Thien's weight pulled it rapidly back through the pulley. He plunged toward the floor only to stop abruptly when Doug and Jan snubbed the rope, instantly interrupting his fall.

Inertia took over. The two weights attached to his ankle tried to keep moving floorward. As they did so they dislocated Thien's ankles, knees, hips, vertebrae, and almost wrenched his shoulders from his body. Thien screamed in agony and passed out.

"Vell? Vat you think? Suppose he woke up any guards in ze barracks?"

"I don't know. Let's finish this and then get on with our business."

They got the hose that Thien kept at the ready in the room to use to force water down the nostrils and throats of recalcitrant prisoners. Drowning in the flow of water, the treatment was usually enough to gain their cooperation. They opened the valve and played the stream of water on the unconscious man until he shook his head and opened his eyes.

"Colonel Thien. Welcome back. Do you know if Nebraska Wesleyan has ever won a league playoff?" Then with Doug watching, Szigmond broke both of Thien's legs and gave enough play in the rope to lower him to floor level. Thien achieved new depths of pain. His entire body ached from the fall and sudden stop. He could ease that pain a little if he could put his weight on his legs. That was, however, impossible for both were broken. All he could do in his misery was to scream.

Doug once again took the knife from Szigmond. "One more thing, Colonel. I know you are going to like this one." He put a small nick in one of the veins in Thien's wrist. The colonel could feel the blood flowing down over his hands and fingers and dripping onto the floor.

"You are going to bleed to death Colonel, unless someone from the barracks hears your screams and happens to come into the building. Too bad you have given orders that they never enter this room except when escorting a prisoner. So even if they come in downstairs I doubt they will be coming up here. I wonder what effect that is going to have on you now, you murdering bastard?"

Thien sobbed in pain and humiliation. From somewhere deep within his agony he managed to hiss: "You will . . . never be able . . .

74

to escape. . . My men will . . . hunt you down and . . . kill you both . . . like dogs."

"Let's go now, Captain," Szigmond said urgently. "Many things yet to be done before ve leave here."

They left the interrogation room after Doug took a last look at his tormentor, now tied and trying to stand on broken legs while a widening pool of his blood flowed onto the floor. They could hear Thien's screams long after they closed the door behind them.

Back on the first floor they went down the corridors opening cell doors and urgently calling to the prisoners. "Wake up. Wake up. Thien is dead. The guards are dead. Your cell door is open. Get out of here. Look for supplies. Take what you need and head south. Hurry. Hurry." Some men, still terrified of more torture, simply cowered back on their cots and looked wild-eyed at Doug and Jan. Others stumbled to their feet and staggered from their cells. There began a frenzy among them as they filled the corridors and milled about, unsure what to do next. Lieutenant Colonel Jerry Corley, the ranking officer, tried to organize the newly freed POWs, but they were ill or confused or desperately searching for items that might help them as they tried to escape. There was little the Colonel could do. He managed to convince five or six men to stay with him, but the rest scattered in all directions. Doug never saw any of them again.

Several of those men who were released shook hands with Doug and Jan or hugged them. "Thank you," they cried. "Oh God, thank you."

Having opened all the cells, Jan and Doug left the building and moved quietly toward the storage shed where Szigmond kept his treasures. They stayed in the shadows as much as possible in hopes that no restless guard would come out of the barracks and glimpse them and sound an alarm. They *had* to get away from this place before that happened. Otherwise they stood no chance.

They stood inside the shadowy shack lit only by a single candle Jan had set up on a small table. They surveyed his goods and decided that some items were superfluous. They had to have maps. They had to have back packs. Weapons and ammunition were essential. They strapped 9mm pistols around their waists, picked up AK-47 rifles and slipped the carrying straps over their shoulders. They dug into Jan's stockpile of food and crammed their backpacks full. Then they walked through the compound on their way to its gate. They passed several of the POWs and told them about Szigmond's cache of supplies. They were free to take anything that might help them.

As they cleared the gate, Doug thought back to a sermon he had once heard his friend, Chaplain (Major) Paul Eastley give.

"You remember Chaplain Eastley, don't you Jan?" he asked.

"Yess, very vell."

"Well, he preached to us once on something from the Bible that tells people to 'shake off the dust from your feet as you leave that house or town.' By god, that's what we are doing. Shaking off the dust from the cells, the guards, and from Colonel Thien. And it feels damn good." The two men disappeared into the shades of night, both well aware that their journey would require them to cross something like two hundred miles before they were once more safe inside American-held territory.

* * * * *

CHAPTER FIVE

"For lo, the winter is past, the rain is over and gone, the flowers appear on the earth, the time of singing has come, and the voice of the turtle is heard in our land."-- Song of Solomon II: 11-12.

That June day in 1969 was perfect, Nancy thought. It was so special she was glad she had taken a thirty day leave from her army nurse duties at Fort Sam Houston in San Antonio, Texas. Now she was back in Huron, Ohio, the town that had been her home for her first eighteen years. An azure sky overhead was interrupted by fluffy clouds. Flowers bloomed in profusion along the walkways to the Saints Peter and Paul Missouri Synod Lutheran Church. The air was balmy, filled with the scents of late spring. The temperature hovered at just over 80 degrees. Nancy was pleased that her wedding was to be in the afternoon. It gave her time beforehand to get ready and time after the service for entertaining guests and still getting started on her honeymoon before nightfall. These thoughts filled her mind as she stood in an anteroom of the church, waiting for the moment when, escorted by her father, she would walk out the door and into a new life.

Even now her Jonathan and his best man, his brother David, were standing at the front of the church, below the altar, waiting for her maid of honor, Laura Andrews, to walk up the aisle, reach her position, turn and expectantly wait for the bride. Soon Nancy West would disappear forever and, like a moth emerging from its chrysalis, Nancy would walk out of the church as Mrs. Jonathan Diedrich. The only thing dampening her enthusiasm was the unbidden recollection that, once upon a year, she had planned to become Mrs. Douglas MacArthur Andrews. She mouthed a short prayer for the repose of his soul, freed now long ago from his body on some forgotten Vietnamese battlefield.

Nancy's memories of Doug were still precious to her. For that reason and because of the times they had lain in one another's arms, she had decided not to be married in virginal white. It was a way of honoring one man while giving herself to another. Now 27 years old and still with the body of a young girl, Nancy was lovely in her bridal gown of candlelight white, an off-white golden color, that fell to the floor with a three foot train. The lower part of the gown was covered with seed pearls. It was cut in a simple style with straight princess lines and had short capped sleeves. She wore elbow length gloves to match her gown. Fastened down the back with covered buttons, it was cut very low in the bodice, allowing her to show not only decolletage but the beautiful golden cross inherited from her grandmother.

Nancy wore a fingertip veil with a tiara of pearls and with more seed pearls along its bottom. For her shoes she had chosen medium length heels dyed to match her dress. She wore her hair severely pulled back and done into a French braid. She had to smile at how she had followed tradition. A traditional blue garter. A borrowed strapless bra from a friend. Grandma's cross for the old. And of course her bridal gown for the new.

It was time. The organist swelled the registers in front of her and the massive pipe organ rolled out the first notes of Wagner's "Wedding March." With her father holding her arm, Nancy started down the aisle. Nancy was happy to be escorted by her father. He certainly was not a distinguished looking man–potbellied and wearing a suit that did nothing to disguise it, short, bald–but he was her father and she loved him dearly.

Father and daughter passed her mother, a quiet plain woman, dressed in clothes Nancy had picked out for her, seated there with Nancy's elderly grandmother. Her mother dabbed at her eyes with a handkerchief and smiled at her beloved daughter, her only child. She and her husband had been so pleased when she was born. They raised her in this very church and she had always been faithful in attendance and in participation in youth activities. She had gone off to college and then to nurse's training and so they saw very little of her. But their love for one another continued unabated. They had eagerly read her letters from Viet Nam telling of the infantry officer she had met. She told them how she and Doug loved one another and planned to marry. She even sent a sketch of her engagement ring. They felt useless and powerless to help their daughter in her inconsolable grief when word came that he had been killed in action, only a few days before he was to return to the States. Mother and father wondered for a time whether she would ever conquer her desolation, but then letters began to arrive telling of an acquaintance she had made with a pharmaceutical salesman. Now they would see her wed that man this day.

As she and her father walked down the aisle, Nancy saw Jonathan standing in front of her, waiting for her to join him. He wore a suit recently made specially for him by Richards Clothiers of Tampa. He was very handsome, his soft curly brown hair and his six foot height pulled at her heartstrings. She was lucky indeed. He smiled at her and she thought he looked very handsome. She knew he had put his pharmaceutical sales position on hold so he could join her here and begin their marriage in her own home town and home church. He might have been able to argue her into getting married in San Antonio in a civil wedding. But he had not. Instead he had looked forward to seeing Huron and meeting her parents and seeing the church she had attended for so many years.

She came to her appointed place. Laura Andrews, holding a bouquet, came to stand beside her. The pastor intoned the words: "Who gives this woman in marriage?" and her father replied "I do," and took her hand and placed it in Jonathan's, before retreating to his seat in the front pew beside her mother and grandmother.

* * * * *

Chalmers and Charlotte Andrews sat in a pew near the front of the sanctuary not far behind the West family and they felt the organ music wash over them. They smiled as they saw their daughter Laura in her bridesmaid dress walk to the front to the strains of Lohengrin and stand there expectantly, waiting for Nancy's arrival. They watched Nancy and her father proceed up the aisle.

Charlotte leaned close to Chalmers. "Oh Dad, she is so very pretty. Her gown is lovely. I am happy for her, but I so wished she could have become our daughter-in-law."

79

Chalmers fingered the University of South Florida class ring taken from the body of his son. It had been crushed and was missing its stone when he was given it. He had gone to the town jeweler who reconstructed it to look like new. He wore it constantly and now he rubbed it almost as if it were Aladdin's Lamp. He too wished things could have been different. Every day of his life now there was an ache in his heart upon awakening and throughout the day and often at night he dreamed of his shattered hopes that someday Doug was going to become the head of the Andrews family. It would have been so joyous for him to have been able to bounce grandchildren on his lap and put them to bed and play ridiculous, childish games with them. Now that would never happen unless Laura married and she presently seemed uninterested in doing so. Even if she had children, they would not bear the Andrews' name. The family line that had played such a prominent role in Nebraska history would end with Chalmers.

Nevertheless, feeling Charlotte's sorrow, he leaned close and whispered in her ear. "I love you honey. It's o.k. We'll get through this." He knew that, for him at least, it was a lie but Charlotte smiled at him and seemed to relax a little.

* * * * *

"Dearly beloved, we are gathered together here in the sight of God, and in the face of this company, to join together this man and this woman in holy matrimony, instituted by God for the comfort and help of his children and so that families might be trained in goodness and godliness of life."

Nancy felt Jonathan's shoulder pressing against her and his hand squeezed hers as they listened to the pastor intone the traditional words of the marriage ceremony.

"If anyone can show cause why these two should not be blessed and joined together, speak now or forever hold your peace."

Nancy's heart raced. She knew no one would speak up. It just wasn't done. The words were simply part of an ancient formula. Yet momentarily she wondered whether she should announce to all assembled that a part of her still loved Douglas MacArthur Andrews?

She knew she could not do that either. It would break Jonathan's heart and would do nothing to banish the ghost that haunted her.

The pastor turned toward the groom. "Jonathan Diedrich, will you have this woman as your wife, to live in God's holy estate of matrimony? Will you love her, comfort her, honor and keep her in sickness and in health, forsaking all others, as long as you both shall live?"

Jonathan's voice was clear and crisp. "Yes, I will."

The pastor looked at Nancy and asked her the same questions. Her answer was tremulous and quiet. "Yes."

At the pastor's quiet direction, Jonathan took Nancy's right hand with his own. They both looked expectantly at him.

"Say after me . . . ."

And Jonathan repeated the ancient pledge. Now it was Nancy's turn. As he had done with Jonathan, now the pastor broke the vow into short phrases so that Nancy could follow it and recite it without becoming confused.

"I, Nancy Elaine West . . . take thee, Jonathan Barr Diedrich . . . to be my wedded husband . . . to have and to hold from this day forward . . . for better for worse . . . for richer for poorer . . . in sickness and in health . . . to love and to cherish . . . till death us do part . . . according to God's holy ordinance . . . and thereto I give thee my troth."

The couple loosed hands and Jonathan turned to his brother David and held out his hand. The groomsman handed him a ring. Jonathan turned to Nancy and said to her as he slipped it on her finger "With this ring I thee wed; in the Name of the Father, and of the Son, and of the Holy Ghost. Amen."

Now Nancy turned to Laura, received a ring from her, and repeated to Jonathan the words he had said to her.

The pastor prayed.

"Oh, eternal our God, king of the universe and giver of every good and perfect gift, we give thee thanks this day for the lives of Nancy and Jonathan and ask your blessing upon their union in holy matrimony."

Then he urged them once again to hold hands and looked over their heads to those in the audience.

"Forasmuch as Nancy and Jonathan have consented together in holy wedlock and have witnessed the same before God and this company, and have pledged to each other their troth, by the Apostolic authority given me by this Holy Church of Christ, and by the laws of this State, I pronounce that they are man and wife, in the Name of the Father, and of the Son, and of the Holy Ghost. Amen."

"Those whom God hath joined together let no man put asunder."

Once again the organ swelled with the strains of the traditional wedding march as Jonathan and Nancy, holding hands, walked swiftly back down the aisle to the rear of the sanctuary where they stopped to receive congratulations by friends and relatives.

* * * * *

When Chalmers and Charlotte reached the happy couple, Charlotte felt a tear escape her eye but she quickly rubbed it away, smiled, and kissed Nancy on the cheek. "I know you will be very happy, my dear." Chalmers silently shook Jonathan's hand, unable in his emotional state to get a single syllable past his choked up vocal chords. Then he gave Nancy a hug–a last hug. They passed out of the church and stood with other guests. Chalmers looked at his wife. "Honey, come on. Let's leave. Neither of us is very happy and we don't want to rain on their parade. Laura is here to uphold the family honor." He smiled at his small joke. "She has her own rental car. She can get back to the airport by herself. You and I? We need to be by ourselves. Besides, we would have to wait through photographs, through the opening of presents and through the cutting of the cake. I am just not up to it. We don't need to see her open our gift of the Lasting Spring silver." Charlotte nodded and they moved quietly to their parked rental and drove back to their hotel.

* * * * *

Two thousand miles and more away, Chaplain Paul Eastley sat in his spartan room in the bachelor officers' quarters at the Presidio, blissfully unaware that Nancy had just married Jonathan Diedrich.

82

Nancy had asked him months earlier to officiate, but he had begged off, pleading the press of his military duties. Earlier that day Paul had paged listlessly through a journal he had kept during his year in Viet Nam and had glanced across the entries, stopping occasionally to read some of them carefully. He read again how Ron Mattle had been killed by a booby trap placed by some Viet Cong. He remembered the inept medic Willie Moore and how he had written a recommendation that he be placed into a job he could handle more easily. He recalled how he had gone on a sweep with Doug Andrews' unit and how he had captured an officer of the North Vietnamese Army who was calling artillery down on them and how poor Private Harry Kinback had climbed a tall tree, the better to see enemy movements and to snipe at them. He had died up there and Paul could still see his blood slowly dripping from the tree and congealing on the ground. Paul thought he was probably the only chaplain in all the years of the conflict in Viet Nam who had ever captured an enemy soldier.

With a snap of his wrist he closed the journal and laid it on his desk. This was not a day to feel remorse or sorrow or bitterness for lost comrades or to entertain any other negative emotion. Today was his day. Just that morning he had learned that the promotion board in St. Louis had reached far down below the zone and had promoted him from lieutenant colonel to full colonel. A full bull. A bird colonel. A chicken colonel. He didn't care what others might call his rank. The eagle with spread wings was the most beautiful of all army rank insignia and the pay raise was significant. He smiled. He was now so high in rank there was hardly anyone left for him to salute. The only negative he could see was that this promotion would probably cause him to be reassigned away from the Presidio. He had loved it here with its Pacific winds, its fog, its cold damp temperatures, and its old buildings that had housed so many adventures over the decades. He stood up and walked to the mirror, studied his face therein and laughed. He gave himself a playful salute. "Let the good times roll," he thought.

* * * * *

83

It was now evening time and Colonel Paul sat with friends and well wishers in the bar of the officer's club at the Presidio. An old military custom–the promotion party–dictated that he should invite friends and co-workers to the club for a drink and for merry making. As a chaplain he was opposed to the use of strong liquors, but he had no compunction about wine, and so he had ordered the bar to lay in a supply of various sweet and dry wines. There were fake howls of protest from his buddies who were used to stronger medicine. Despite that, they seemed to like what Paul had provided and the wines were quickly disappearing as time slipped by.

Paul sat under a hastily made, sad-looking banner that proclaimed: "Best wishes to Colonel Paul." Helium-filled balloons floated in the air. Twists of crepe paper were taped to the walls. Laughter and loud conversation filled the room as his guests broke into small groups to chat with one another. Around Paul gathered most of those he had come to know since his arrival at the Presidio two years before.

One man, a little tipsy, regaled Paul with a vision of his future.

"Why, hell Paul, you doin' so well for the army and the chaplaincy, goin' so fast up the rank ladder, that you could be promoted to brigadier general if you keep on workin' hard and keepin' your nose clean. Hell boy, they might even make you chief of chaplains some day!! Or at least the assistant chief."

"I think he is called the deputy chief, Vic, and I don't believe there is any chance of those things happening. Most chiefs come from liturgical churches like the Anglican or Lutheran or even Methodist. Occasionally there have been Roman Catholics and once there was a black Baptist, but that was a fluke. There's never been a chief from a real non-liturgical denomination like mine. I don't think a free church Congregationalist would stand much chance of getting the top job, Vic. But hey, boy, at least your heart is in the right place. Maybe some day you can vote me into the top job?'

One of his friends from the headquarters personnel section came up to Paul a little later and spoke in a low tone. "Paul? I suppose

I should let it wait a day or two until you are notified through proper channels, but it's too good to keep to myself."

"What's up?" Paul rejoined.

"The word just came down. We received it just minutes before we closed up for the day. Would you like to know where you are going? What your next duty assignment will be?"

"Sure. Who wouldn't?"

"Well, you'll be here a couple of more weeks and then you are to report to the Army Chaplain Center and School at Fort Wadsworth, New York."

"I wonder why they want me?"

"Get real, Paul. You are one of the best chaplains in the Corps. Your record is a stellar one. And how many chaplains wear the hero gongs you do–two purple hearts, a bronze star, a silver star? Plus your jump wings, the Ranger tab, and then the attaboys like your expert rifle badge, your cute little hanger proclaiming you expert in pistol, grenade and machine gun? I'll tell you why they want you. They want you because you are good! They want you not only because you are a good officer. They appreciate you because you are a man of deep Christian faith. And they want you to become Commandant of the Chaplain School! I've said it before, Paul. Keep this up and one day they will have to seriously consider you for the job of Chief of Chaplains."

Paul could not keep the look of bewilderment off his face, slowly replaced by a foolish grim. "Me? Commandant? Well I guess I will have my work cut out for me." He slapped his friend on the shoulder. "Thanks, guy. Really appreciate you telling me."

Alone in his room later, Paul thought back over the years of his life. He remembered the poverty in which he had been raised after the death of his father. His years of growing up in Central City, Nebraska and his youthful wildness were still fresh in his mind. He still clearly remembered being pulled off some guy in an alley behind the laundry by the town constable, 'Hoot' Gibson, who grumbled "Paul, is there any boy in this town you haven't been in a fight with?" He played football because of the anger that always seemed to simmer just below the surface and it gave him pleasure to smash into some ball carrying opponent and bring him crashing to the ground. He still heard the voice of one of his teachers reverberating in his mind: "Paul, by the time you are thirty you will either be dead or in prison!"

That didn't happen. Instead after his graduation from high school, the president of a tiny local Quaker school, Nebraska Central College, took an interest in him for some obscure reason and arranged for him to receive a tuition and books fellowship paid for by some family back east. His college career lasted only a few weeks. It was difficult to get passing grades when he didn't turn in assignments, didn't take tests, and didn't attend classes. Disgusted with himself and the world, Paul dropped out of NCC and went out to face the world. Now he worked at a variety of jobs as he tried to get a handle on his life and decide what he wanted to do with the years that stretched ahead: scooping snow from sidewalks and driveways, farm hand, cattle ranch hand, janitor in an old people's home, dish washer, soda jerk, power line construction, railroad bridge and builder gang where his job was known as being a 'tunnel rat,' weather stripping windows in a large lumber yard, café waiter, short order cook. Those first two years had been a kaleidoscope of jobs.

Then a close friend talked Paul into trying college once again and he reluctantly agreed to enroll in another tiny school, this time one located in Kansas. Now came two years of college that he was barely able to afford–he had no one to help defray expenses–until he received a certificate of completion from Friends Bible College. Then came his stint in the Army Medical Service Corps, trained as an aidman but working as a clerk. After two years as an enlisted man, he was discharged and returned to FBC to complete a bachelor of theology, this time studying under the G.I. Bill which paid most of his expenses. Now caught up with the challenge of learning, he went on to earn a Master of Science from Fort Hays Kansas State College and a Ph.D. from the University of Kansas.

Somewhere in those years, Paul developed a deep and abiding Christian faith. His majors were philosophy and religious studies and so he was invited to preach by two different small churches, one in

86

Kansas, one in Nebraska. He was ordained by council vicinage while pastoring the eighty-five member Congregational Church in Ashland, Nebraska. It was while he served there that he decided to join the Nebraska National Guard. Feeling that he needed more of a challenge in his life, Paul applied for and was accepted into active duty. That year was 1964 and hardly anyone had yet heard of Viet Nam.

Paul attended the Chaplain Officer Basic Course at Fort Hamilton, New York, on the tip of Brooklyn and only a subway ride away from all the free shows an army officer could attend on Broadway, just by showing up at the USO ticket office on Times Square and asking for tickets. He was unsatisfied when he completed the basic course. It was as if he could not complete a sufficient number of military schools. While most of his fellows went on to chaplain assignments upon completion of the basic course, Paul volunteered for Jump School at Fort Benning. When he graduated, it was off to Ranger School. The course began at Fort Benning. Fifty-eight eighteen hour days. Then to Camp Darby, Camp Frank Merrill, and Camp James E. Rudder to complete his training.

Only then did he feel he had learned enough to function as an effective chaplain, a friend, guide and helper to enlisted men and a counselor to officers. Thereafter he would always feel that his days as an enlisted man were as leaven to the biblical lump. They made it possible for him to understand the stresses and strains that enlisted men were subjected to. Often those stresses were unfair or could be avoided by a little attention paid to them by those of higher rank. Now he had the authority and knowledge to step in and correct them when he saw fit to do so. Then, after a short tour of duty at Fort Monroe, Virginia, he was off to Viet Nam. It was early 1966. During almost his entire time in-country he was assigned to the 2nd Battalion, 11th Infantry Brigade (Separate), 23rd Infantry Division, save for a final posting to Saigon of a few months before his tour ended.

Twice he came close to death, once when a grenade was thrown into his jeep, killing his driver and leaving a cicatrice of scars around his left eye. Then there were the body scars left by the ambush at Landing Zone Yankee near Chu Pong mountain when so many of his charges died in the opening fusillade from the hidden enemy. A platoon ambushed by a company. It was no contest. He had taken refuge behind a headstone in the nearby cemetery along with the Radio Telephone Operator. He took the handset from the RTO and called in help: gunships, artillery, medevac flights. It was while carrying injured men from the battlefield to the dust-off helicopters that he had been shot, once in the leg, once in the shoulder. But he had managed to save eleven men who might otherwise have died. Later there was talk of a Medal of Honor for him, but opposition by the Chief of Chaplains caused the award to be downgraded to a Silver Star.

Paul thought of all the friends he had made among the troops with which he served there in Viet Nam, and of those who had died in that pointless, misbegotten war pushed so avidly by his government. First there had been Kennedy whom he had admired so much at first. Then came Lyndon Johnson who seemed to believe the war was a personal contest with Ho Chi Minh. Richard Nixon was beginning a campaign for the presidency and showed no signs of willingness to end the war. It often surprised him that what he saw there did not entirely destroy his faith in Christ and God. That had not happened. Instead his time there had been one of spiritual growth for him as he nurtured the hurts and Christian faith of those he worked with. He had listened to confessions of sin, to expressions of faith, to prayers asking for Christ's salvation. He had baptized many of his troops. He had listened to gossip and squelched rumors and participated in an endless variety of conversations. His work filled him with a sense of accomplishment. Consequently, Paul extended his time there for a few months, so it was the end of 1967 before he returned to "the World." His first stateside posting was to Fort Riley, Kansas. Then he went to the Presidio in California. Now, it appeared, he would go to Fort Wadsworth, New York, to head up the training for his Corps.

In the midst of his ruminations the hour had grown late. Tomorrow would be a busy day for him. As had been his custom since childhood, Chaplain (Colonel) Paul Eastley knelt beside his bed and there prayed for his country, for himself, and for all those whose spiritual welfare were his prime responsibility.

"O Lord of souls, you have called me to service in your Church. Use me as it pleases you for the glory of your name. Make my will pliant to yours. Empty me of self and fill me with the meekness of wisdom. Mellow my judgment, stir my zeal, enlarge my heart, increase my faith. Let my life reflect what my lips utter. Be with my leaders, my charges, my loved ones. Make us all faithful and at the last, give us the crown of life, through Jesus Christ our Lord. Amen."

* * * * *

CHAPTER SIX

"For everything there is a season . . . . a time to kill . . . . a time to break down . . . . a time to cast away . . . . a time to rend . . . . a time to hate . . . . a time for war . . . ."–Ecclesiastes III: 1-8 <u>passim</u>.

Their clothes were in rags but Doug and Jan had managed to keep their weapons clean and oiled. As Jan had said, they could reach American lines naked if they were forced to do so, but they would hardly be able to do so if they had unusable rusted weapons and they encountered human obstacles. The food they brought from the prison lasted nearly two weeks, supplemented occasionally by some small animal caught in one of Szigmond's snares. After that they had to forage for their food. Szigmond knew of some edible plants and even when bitter were rapidly consumed due to their hunger. From time to time they were able to gather and husk rice from isolated paddies.

They lay now in a bamboo thicket watching the activity in the tiny hamlet just ahead. A buffalo boy dozed on the back of his animal. A child of perhaps six herded a small flock of geese. Women and men worked in nearby rice fields and the elderly took their ease in front of their hooches working on small tasks. The two men waited for the sunset and the approach of full night. There was no moon and they knew they could safely move forward as long as they were careful.

As Szigmond whispered to Andrews, they had been traveling for nearly three weeks. They had escaped from the prison in late 1969. He thought they had averaged perhaps four to five miles each night. If his calculations were correct they had moved from eighty to one hundred miles closer to American lines. In the first days after they fled the prison they repeatedly had to hunker down in whatever cover they could find as soldiers in squad-sized groups searched the countryside for them. Sometimes those soldiers had come close to spotting them and only plain blind dumb luck kept them from being seen and killed or recaptured. The same was not true for other less fortunate prisoners.

For some days after escaping from the prison, Jan and Doug were aware of different men, singly or in bands, working their way south. They were close enough to see how when recaptured, North Vietnamese soldiers often shot them on the spot. Others the soldiers chose to return to the prison where they might be brutally interrogated in an attempt to learn who had instigated the break out, and who it was who might have tortured and murdered Colonel Thien. Grim gallows humor entertained them during hours of forced inaction as they lay under cover from prying eyes. At least, if they were recaptured, they joked to one another, Colonel Thien would not be the one to interrogate them, the blood that had dripped from his wrist prevented that. Both men talked about how nice it would have been to be able to stay and watch Thien die. But that was long ago. It had been many days now since Doug and Jan had seen evidence of other prisoners, still free and still moving south. They came to believe that they were the only ones left and that fact made them extremely cautious. They knew that one tiny slip was all that was necessary to cause them to fail. The days passed and they remained free. Doug thought that they had been free of the prison for something like one hundred days, three months. If so, now it was about September 1969.

Szigmond insisted that they travel in bounding overwatch fashion and Doug saw the wisdom of doing so. They would both remain under cover until absolutely certain no watching eyes were near. Then they would select the next hiding place, perhaps only a few yards away, perhaps some distance from their current position. Then one man would move quickly to that selected spot while the first covered his advance. Then the rear guard would come forward protected by the rifle of the lead man. It made for slow going, but it was the safest way to move. These movements reminded Andrews of the ROTC tactical exercise years before when as a University of South Florida college senior he, Rassmussen and Galusha had moved cross country in bounding overwatch. They had been captured but because he was some distance behind them, the cadre had not spotted him. Now, here in Viet Nam, perhaps that might happen again. If either he or Jan were unlucky enough to be seen while moving forward, the other might still be safe and could continue his southward march.

At first Szigmond had to expend a great deal of energy helping the wounded officer from place to place. Doug was still weak from his prison mistreatment and try as he would, it was difficult for him with his grotesquely healed feet to continue toward their goal so far away. More than once he suggested that Jan leave him and go on alone. Such comments brought only a grunt from the Pole. Then as the days passed, Doug's feet, abused and beaten by the bamboo rod as Thien interrogated him, began to bother him less. He was surprised that they were healing at all, much less improving. Now he did not hobble nor stagger as much as formerly.

It was a worthwhile improvement. The food they carried was long since gone and now both men were suffering from hunger, from malnutrition, and from the ever-present intestinal parasites. Whenever they had to cross a paddy or stream they were assailed by leeches that gathered on them to feast. Doug detested the creatures. As they moved south these problems made it increasingly difficult even for Szigmond to keep himself moving, much less offer aid to Andrews. If they had not had each other to encourage and strengthen, neither would have been able to remain free. And so they continued on their way.

Doug and Jan sometimes staggered through lush jungle growth which tore at them and impeded their movement. They stumbled and fell across tree roots. They forced their way through fields of elephant grass taller than they. They crawled carefully through open savannah country and struggled through swamps with heavy mud clumping to their shoes. They wormed their way through bamboo thickets. At one low point, Jan sat beside a rancid stream and bathed his companion's face with fetid water. They traveled at night and so guided themselves by the stars and by the map that Jan had scrounged before they fled the prison. He regularly stopped for a moment to orient the map to the contours of the land.

They walked forcing themselves onward. When they stopped to rest they felt the waves of pain that tortured muscles sent throughout their bodies. Time after time, as they had pushed themselves to the limits of their strength, they sagged to the ground for a moment's rest. Such stops were all too rare, making them even more precious. It was a luxury to sit down, to stretch their legs, to lean back against a tree and relax. They found that getting back up was difficult. All the while they had slumped on the ground their muscles had twitched and spasmed. Once back on their feet it took some moments for them to shake off the aches and pains they felt before they could again push forward, staggering on deadened feet.

They slept, huddling on the ground without blankets or ponchos, receiving the brunt of rainstorms that sometimes drenched them. Doug discovered that no matter how hard he pushed his body beyond normal limits, it would still respond. His mind was another matter. After hours of doggedly putting one foot in front of the other, his mind shut down, its ability to reason and solve problems gone. Only another few hours of rest could even slightly restore it. Both Doug and Jan realized how really spent they were. They knew they were physically and mentally exhausted, but they refused to give up. To surrender would mean their deaths.

When they began their trek they wore boots. Mildew and damp soon began rotting them. That was bad enough to feel their footgear falling away. Even worse was the constant wet that plagued their feet. The skin, wet long enough, began to peel and then to slough away. Doug and Jan both knew they were in the first stages of foot immersion sickness, first noticed by the Army in the Great War of 1914-1918 and then called trench foot. They managed to make sandals for themselves and threw their boots away. Now, although their feet continued to get wet on a regular basis, at least they could dry off between times.

After the first few days of their flight from prison they were always hungry. They felt so famished that when they encountered a wild hog in the jungle, Jan managed to kill it with his homemade Randall knife. They built a tiny fire and cooked strips of meat, then stuffing them into their mouths and swallowing while grease ran down their chins and into their lengthening beards. They stayed at that camp for three days while they tried to save most of the hog meat by grilling it on the fire. It lasted them for some days as they continued on their way but eventually they had to discard the last of it, now crawling with maggots and giving off an unpleasant odor.

Day after day their minds fixated on food. Doug fashioned a bamboo spear. As they closed on one hamlet a mongrelly community dog came growling toward them. Both fearful of being discovered and hungry, Doug killed it with his spear. By turns, each carried the carcass for some distance before they felt it was safe to stop. Then, as they had the hog, they butchered the dog and roasted its meat.

They decided that dog meat was not objectionable and that it both satisfied their hunger and gave them strength. Thereafter, whenever possible, they dined on community dogs. Anything to keep them going south. To vary their diet, Doug demonstrated to Jan how to take a hen out of its roost in the branches of a tree without wakening it and thus arousing those in a nearby house.

"I learned this when I was a kid and spent time on my uncle's farm," Doug said. "He wanted me to get the hens out of the trees and into the hen house, so I fashioned a hook at the end of a coat hangar and reached up to try to hook their leg and thus be able to pull them out of the tree. That roused them and they squawked and carried on. The cries of the first one caused the others to flutter higher into the tree or fly to the ground and run off in all directions. So my uncle showed me a better way. He had me climb the tree til the birds were within reach. Then he showed me how to slip fingers under their breasts as they clung to a branch. They would sleepily climb from the branch onto my finger without a sound. Then I could hand them down to my uncle who put them into a sack and after getting several, we would take them and put them away in the hen house." That method worked as well in Viet Nam as it had in Nebraska and they regularly ate stolen chicken.

Although they had found ways to combat their hunger, they still grew cynical about their chances of reaching American lines. They had only a slight hope as they pushed south, night after endless night, laying in hiding during daylight hours. At last they even ceased speculating as to whether or not they would be able to survive and

95

reach their destination. It came to be no more than an ephemeral dream, yet still they continued, knowing that they were subject to being attacked and recaptured at any point.

It was that fear that kept them from using their weapons. Not once had they found it necessary to fire a single shot from either rifle or pistol. Both men realized that a rifle report would pinpoint their location. Local people would report what they had heard to higher authorities. They had to remain invisible if they were to succeed. Still, knowing that one day they might have to use them, they kept their rifles well preserved with gun oil Jan had scrounged while they were both in the prison.

Sometimes they could follow trails and occasionally, for a short distance, they used the primitive roads they came across. More often they walked across country, through forests of bamboo, through chest high elephant grass leaving a susurrus behind them as they passed, through meadows, through rice paddies. Using a trail or road was a great relief after a strenuous hike through the countryside. Yet that was also where they faced the greatest danger of being discovered by anyone who might be out looking for them or by some enemy soldier who by chance might encounter and challenge them. And so, when an open stretch lay before them, they carefully eyed it trying to find the best way to cross it. Then they ran for their lives toward the next bit of cover. Their weakened bodies allowed only for painfully slow progress as sweat streamed out of their pores and their lungs burned for oxygen.

Whenever possible they avoided even the smallest of the many hamlets they saw, giving them a wide berth. They stole past hundreds of such settlements, each one potentially capable of ruining their plan to escape. Most of them were much alike–a central dusty street, fifteen or twenty shacks built upon poles to keep them dry during monsoon season, a communal well, a brightly painted pagoda as colorful as a Faberge egg, and animal pens. Ducks waddled along waterways. Chickens clucked and scratched in the dirt. Water buffalo lowed in their night corals. It was essential that they get past such communities without wakening sleepers and without being seen by the occasional insomniac.

They slowly moved south through the sloppy wet weather as the weeks went by, putting an ever increasing number of kilometers behind them. Thirty. Fifty. One hundred. One hundred and twenty.

* * * * *

One evening while preparing for their night movement, Doug roused himself from his usual stupor in an effort to postpone their departure. Even after sleeping he was still dead on his feet. Perhaps a little conversation would do the trick. He looked at Jan and said, "You know? We are following the example set down by the early Vietnamese as they colonized their coastal nation and overran a couple of other cultures in the process, like the Cambodians and the Champans. They started out in the Ha Noi region and headed south. As they moved further away from Ha Noi in generation after slow generation, they called their movement the 'Southward March.' Jan, I guess that's what we're doing; making a southward march. Let's hope it doesn't take us as long as it did the Vietnamese. From Ha Noi to the Ca Mau peninsula in the south took them over five hundred years! I don't think we have that much time left." Szigmond gave a rare smile but his only comment was "It has been a hell of a day." They shouldered their packs and moved out. Soon, as always, they were soaked with sweat as they continued their trek toward a place of safety.

Sometimes they could hear the crump of bomb explosions not too far away. They discussed those noises and concluded that they were caused by unseen Air Force B-52s flying too high to be seen, dropping their bombs on tactical or strategic targets. Szigmond cynically told Doug that in most cases they were simply unloading their explosives so they wouldn't have to go back to Guam and try to land with their deadly cargo still on board. Both men hoped they wouldn't find themselves one day at ground zero.

During one night march, as they followed along a primitive trail, Doug noticed a suspicious spot just ahead of them on the path. He was following Jan and, without further consideration, threw himself against his comrade, knocking him to the side and onto the ground.

"Sorry, Jan. I thought I saw something."

Doug rose and moved toward the darkened spot on the path.

"Look. By God, look. Come here, Jan!"

Szigmond stood and walked to where his friend stood. By the time he got there, Doug had kicked aside some leafy cover and they stared down into a dark hole. At the bottom both could see sharpened bamboo stalks buried in the dirt with their points raised. It was a punji pit and it was a miracle that both had been spared the agony of falling onto those stakes, the points smeared with human or animal feces the better to induce infections in the unwary.

Szigmond dipped his head in laconic thanks. "That's why I brought you along, Captain."

They wondered why anyone had dug such a pit that far north. Surely it wasn't meant to entrap ARVN or American soldiers. They concluded finally that it might be a training aid used by the northern enemy. On they went, a little more carefully.

On another night they heard the sound of walking men and quickly moved into hiding where they breathlessly crouched and watched while an entire company of enemy soldiers moved in single file past them. When they were gone both Doug and Jan heaved sighs of relief. Before resuming their march, Jan told Doug that the episode had given him an idea.

Several nights later the incident was repeated. Once again Doug and Jan leaped to the side of the trail they had been following and crawled into the underbrush there. They waited as they heard the sound of walking feet moving closer and the occasional whispered tonal comment. Jan waited patiently until the last man had passed and had moved perhaps ten meters down the trail. Then he crept forward with knife in hand, closed the distance with the man in front of him, reached out, his hand covering the other's mouth, and cut his throat. The man's body sagged without a sound and, yanking off his headcover he tossed it to Doug and then dropped the dead man onto the ground just off the trail. Then, swiftly and silently, he advanced onto the next man and repeated his slaughter. Now both he and Doug had enemy headgear to put on. In the dimness of night it would take a close inspection to discover that they were not who they now pretended to be–the last two men in the column.

Jan's act had been incredibly dangerous, risking their exposure after so many weeks of hardship. Yet that night, from the moment they stepped into line with the others in the column to the time of false dawn the next day they covered more kilometers than they had on any other single night since their escape. As the sky began to lighten in the east, Doug and Jan dropped out of the line of march and went to cover. They hoped that it would still be some time before the soldiers realized that two of their number were gone. It would take much longer to backtrack and discover their bodies. By that time Doug and Jan could be long gone and well hidden.

As they bedded down later, hoping to slow their racing pulses enough to get a little sleep, Szigmond looked at Jan.

"Ve did o.k,, Captain."

"Yes we did, Jan. We were incredibly lucky. Do you remember Bismarck? He once said that God has a special providence for fools, drunkards, and the United States of America. Tonight we got some of that special providence."

It was January 1970 and Captain Douglas MacArthur Andrews had been dead and buried for nearly two years.

* * * * *

As weeks passed and the countryside blossomed with ever more hamlets, Szigmond pointed out that if they continued their march on its present course, they were nearly bound to be spotted, captured, killed. Their only hope, he told Doug, was to begin to angle westward toward the mountains. He told Doug that when he had fought here with the Foreign Legion, those forbidding peaks had been known as "Chaine Annamatique," and the Vietnamese called them "Nui Truong Son."

"If we can get up into the Annamese Corrdilerra, ve vill find people like us who hate the Wietnamese. They are like the Indians of the United States in early years. The only good Indian is a dead one. Many Indians in Wiet Nam! I saw many and worked with some when here as member of Foreign Legion. Live always in hills and

99

mountains. Many names. Nung. T'ai. H'mong. Tho. Man. Dao. Man thien. Trang. Different tribes, but share common hatred of lowlanders. And lowland Wietnamese hate them too. Kill on both sides. If we can reach them, they vill help us, get us further south."

Doug had heard some of those names on earlier occasions but had never given them a second thought until now. They simply had not been within his area of operations and hence were unimportant. No longer. Now they might be a refuge.

Viet Nam is such a narrow country that the Cordillera mountains separating it from Laos and Cambodia are never very far away. They could almost always be seen, and sometimes they twisted east until at places like Da Nang and the Hai Van Pass, called in English the Pass of Clouds, the mountains almost fell into the sea. It took many nights of careful movement before they came even into the foothills.

As they moved forward night after night, Doug was continually surprised at how different these mountains were from those in Colorado he had visited as a boy. Central City itself sat at an elevation of 1,703 feet. He knew. On both sides of the town along Highway 30 road signs proudly announced that fact. Driving west the land continually rose until by the time Denver was reached, the altitude was 5,280–the 'mile high city.' Then the land rose more sharply as one continued west until cresting either Loveland or Berthoud passes. Both were about sixty miles west of Denver. Loveland sat at an elevation of 11,992 while Berthoud was 11,307.

Thus a traveler slowly moved from 1,703 feet to 5,280 feet during a drive of just over 400 miles–a gain of 3,577 feet across land that rose so gently, that a traveler hardly noticed. During the sixty-odd mile drive from Denver to the passes the rise was another 7,000 feet. It took five hundred miles of slowly increasing elevation to move from Central City's 1,703 to Loveland's near 12,000 peak.

The geography of Viet Nam was vastly different. Much of the country was flat land, barely rising out of the South China Sea. The highest point in the eastern part of the country was about 250 feet. Much was lower still. Yet the high point, in Ton Kin was Fan Si Pan mountain at 10,308. The entire Annamese Cordillera rose sharply, without much warning, from the flat lowlands, even though most of it was much lower than Fan Si Pan. Almost everywhere the land rose from sea level to mountain top height in only a very few miles. Doug often thought of this brutal fact during night marches as he and Szigmond forced their exhausted and pain wracked bodies onward.

Finally, when it seemed as if they could go no further, when they were almost ready to surrender even if it meant their execution, they came across a trail that ran generally north/south near the top of the ridge on which they stood. It seemed isolated enough so they followed it. They crossed a second, a third, a fourth, separated by a few kilometers but interwoven, criss-crossed.

Finally Szigmond was convinced. He realized what they had encountered. They were now on the Ho Chi Minh Trail. "It is here that supplies from ze north are carried to ze south. Heavy, brutal labor. All done by hand or bicycle or ox cart. One peasant carries two mortar shells on his back down this trail for two months before reaching allies in the south. He gives zem shells.

"Pt-thong. Pi-thong. Both fired quick. Peasant goes back to trail to start north again to load up with two more mortar shells. Northern general Vo Nguyen Giap has about 200,000 peasants doing such vork."

"Damn, Jan. They are almost as dedicated as we are! Both them and us are going to make it into the south."

Szigmond nodded his head in agreement. They continued south. Sometimes without knowing it they crossed the border into Laos for a time before the trail carried them back into Viet Nam. They occasionally came upon earthen shelters, holes dug in the ground, used by Giap's porters for cover when U.S. planes overhead began dropping bombs on the trail. Regularly, for a time, they encountered such shelters every one hundred yards–just the right distance for coolies to sprint for cover when they heard planes overhead.

Doug thought they must be at about 8,000 feet. Even that high the jungle grew lushly, often completely hiding the network of trails from spying 'eyes in the sky.' They were, however, more concerned with eyes on the ground than with supposed ones in the sky. At places along the trail they saw where northern engineers had laced together the overhanging tops of trees so as to completely hide the trail from overhead searchers. Each dawn they carefully concealed themselves so as to be safe during daylight hours from being spotted by columns of northern Vietnamese moving south. Some of those were soldiers being sent into the Republic of Viet Nam to reinforce their Viet Cong brethren. Doug and Jan both knew they would not be treated kindly if captured.

One night as they struggled southward a short stocky man with a round face suddenly materialized on the trail directly in front of them.

"Bonne nuit," he said.

Doug and Jan crouched and raised their weapons, ready to defend themselves. The strange apparition smiled and gestured toward the jungle hemming the trail on both sides. Doug and Jan could make out half a dozen armed men, moving out of the heavy brush on all sides, some carrying French Lebel rifles, some with cross-bows, some with spears.

Straightening, Jan dropped his rifle to the ground, muttered to Doug to do so also, and replied to the man.

"Bonne nuit, mon chef."

To Doug he whispered that it did no harm to flatter the man by calling him 'chief.'

"Je m'appelle Jan Szigmond. Il est Doug Andrews. Comment allez-vous?"

"Tres bien, merci."

"Mon ami ne comprehends pas Francais et aussi moi un peu. Nous sont Americains."

The little man spoke in English. "Where have you come from? What are you doing here?"

To questions about his ability to speak both French and English, he responded that the French had been in Indo China a long time and almost every adult living there knew at least a little of that language. He had picked up his English while he and his fellows worked with an American Special Forces unit some miles further south as they

102

tried to interdict enemy traffic moving near their camp. He was, he said, named Hoan and he and his people were Nungs, ancient enemies of the Vietnamese. He was glad to learn that they were killers of Vietnamese and that they had escaped from a northern prison. He had never before heard of that happening.

With his men roaming ahead as spotters, Hoan led Doug and Jan by a roundabout way into a small village hidden in the jungle. The community consisted of perhaps a dozen houses, open and airy, setting on poles raising them above the ground, with thatched roofs and carefully fitted mahogany hardwood floors. Nearby sat a blue Buddhist pagoda. In the middle of the buildings was a community well and just outside the hamlet were vegetable gardens. Doug could hear the lowing of a water buffalo.

As they came escorted into the Nung hamlet, old men, women– young and old–and children emerged from the buildings and peered curiously at the two strangely colored men. Hoan talked to them in their native dialect. After a few words, the people seemed to relax and began to smile at Jan and Doug. Hoan busied himself with preparations.

"We must have a welcoming feast."

A pig was slaughtered. Vegetables gathered. Fruits laid out on tables. Home brewed fiery spirits were poured.

"By damn Jan, this is just like a summer church dinner back in Nebraska."

"Good, huh?"

"Damn right."

The two men, half a world away from their homes, ate and drank until they were stuffed and vastly drunk. They sat around the campfire and talked with Hoan as the flames danced and made shadows on their faces. The young girls of the tribe hovered nearby, smiling shyly at them. As embers burned low, Hoan led them to an empty building and showed them where to sleep. Women laid blankets on the floor. In moments, both the men were asleep, comforted by their bellies and by the notion that at last they were among friends.

In the days that followed Doug reveled in the security of the little village. Always its perimeter was guarded by Hoan's men while the rest of the tribe went about their daily activities. Not once did Doug or Jan feel even slightly threatened even though some days they could hear the voices of Vietnamese porters as they moved past down the Ho Chi Minh Trail.

Almost nightly the little community gathered for another feast honoring the two American soldiers. One memory Doug always carried thereafter was the night when everyone sat around the fire eating some kind of stew from a common pot. Hoan turned to Doug, looked into his plate, and said, "My friend, dig a little deeper and get a little more of the puppy on your plate."

After perhaps two weeks–days in the hamlet were timeless–Doug and Jan felt that much of their strength had returned. It was time to go on. When they told Hoan he was saddened, but prepared. He held out to them multi-colored braided and beaded bracelets and tied them around their wrists.

"This is a sign that we will always be brothers."

He and his men escorted Doug and Jan down the trail toward the south, staying with them for several days before they said their final goodbyes and headed back to their hamlet. The two travelers waved their thanks and smiled at one another. The trip that had once seemed endless and impossible, now seemed to be possible and have an end to it. Their strength was greatly renewed as a result of their stay in Hoan's village. They felt fit enough to resume their trek. In two or three more weeks, they might actually cross the magical line of the demilitarized zone and once again be in American territory.

* * * * *

Major Nancy Elaine (West) Diedrich, Nurse Corps, Army Medical Corps, stood at the counter at the nurse's station, fourth floor west, of Brooke Army Medical Center, Fort Sam Houston, Texas. It was late in her shift and she was hoping to finish charting the last of her patients to be seen before it was time for her to leave. She knew she couldn't leave her work undone and she also knew how she loathed to stay past her shift time. She knew that if she were late getting home Jonathan would be upset.

Just then Doctor Jameson paused at the counter.

"Hello, Nancy, you gorgeous creature," he said. "Don't get to see as much of you these days. Too good for us?"

"Oh no, Doctor. It's just that my husband takes up a lot of time and he enjoys having me at home, so I try to get there as quickly as I can."

"Well, you used to stop off at our favorite watering hole and have a drink with the girls and the boys. We miss you."

And with that parting thought, he reached out and put his hand on Nancy's forearm and gave it a friendly squeeze. Perhaps he left his hand on her arm a fractional second longer than necessary. Perhaps not. Nancy never knew. She was only aware at that moment of Jonathan standing a few feet away down the corridor, his eyes burning into hers.

She smiled at him but his face remained frozen in a look of despair, frustration, and anger. Excusing herself from Dr. Jameson, Nancy walked down to where Jonathan stood in the corridor.

"Hi, honey," she began.

He interrupted her with a coarse croak in his voice. "I can't talk about it now," he said. "We will have to settle some things when you get home. I will be there." He turned on his heel and walked away.

He made his last sentence sound like a threat and Nancy felt a chill run down her back.

She felt Dr. Jameson walk up behind her. "Are you o.k., Nancy?" he asked. "Things going alright or is there a problem?"

"I'm sorry, Dr. Jameson. Yes. Things are o.k.," she said with a timid smile on her face. "But I can't talk now. I've got to get home. Bye."

She wheeled her car out of the hospital parking lot and headed for the Memorial bypass that would take her to New Bern, the bedroom community where she and Jonathan lived. As she drove, her mind raced over the past months remembering the signs to which she had given little thought at the time.

* * * * *

Jonathan had always been protective of her since the first time they had met. He wanted, he had told her, to shield her from more hurts.

"You have already suffered enough for two or three people," he told her. His concern for her intensified once they married. Nancy thought his attitude was unhealthy for them both but she learned there was nothing she could do to avoid the problems that soon loomed large. He often expressed his displeasure when she had to work longer than her normal shift. If she got home late there was no welcoming hug or any indication that he was glad they could be together again at the end of this day. Instead he stared coldly at her and for hours at a time remained uncommunicative, stiff, distant. Dinner was eaten in silence.

At night in bed when he made love to her she often felt he was using her rather than sharing a spiritual and physical bond. As her passion and joy dwindled, Jonathan became even more driven in his times of intercourse. Sometimes she felt he was going to pound her down into the mattress. Then he would sigh, roll over on his back and silently fall asleep. He seemed no longer to care whether she reached climax or not. Consequently her interest in sex diminished. More and more she found excuses to stay up after Jonathan went to bed, waiting for him to fall asleep before she slipped in beside him, or to complain she wasn't feeling well, or was too tired. As week after month piled up, Jonathan became ever more frantic to possess her. She knew they should see a marriage counselor but when she suggested it, he grew angry and refused even to consider the idea.

Matters worsened when he began to insinuate that she didn't really love him. He sometimes wondered aloud as to whether or not she had a secret lover. All her protestations did not sway him. He became unsettled when other men looked at her when they were out for an evening. What might have begun as a date, a time for renewal

106

too often degenerated into a one-sided quarrel with her serving as both bait and target. She came to despise the questions Jonathan asked.

"Did you see how that guy was looking at you? He was undressing you with his eyes. Nancy, do you know him?"

Then he began to come suddenly into the den where she often sat while writing her mother and father, or the occasional letter to her friend Laura Andrews, or even the less frequent note to Laura's folks, Chalmers and Charlotte Andrews. He would suspiciously peer over her shoulder while asking plaintively, "Who are you writing to?" When she explained that her letter was to the Andrews, he scoffed. "Why do you want to keep writing to them? They are part of the past. I want you in the here and now. With me. Only with me. I am really all you need. Why not be content with just me?"

All her life she had been close to her mother and father. They had encouraged and supported her in every crisis moment. Jonathan felt threatened even by her love for them and insisted that she not keep in such close contact with them. Horrified by the loss such distancing would cause both her and her parents, Nancy refused.

Then he became fixated on her use of the telephone. While calling a friend, she often heard him pick up an extension so he could listen in on her conversation, presumably to monitor her so that she would be unable to contact her boy friend. When he accused her of such behavior she begged for understanding and pledged that she loved only him, now and always. He remained unconvinced.

Inevitably his temper flared when the telephone rang and he picked up the receiver only to find that the caller hung up at the first sound of his voice. Now he became certain that those occasions were caused by one or another of Nancy's boy friends trying to call her at home to talk to her, perhaps to plan their next meeting. When accused, as she was more often than she once would have thought possible, she cried hopelessly.

"Oh Jonathan, you have got to trust me. I would never betray you. You are my love, my man, my sweetheart. I have no other." When he shrugged off her pleas her tears sometimes turned into wracking sobs. At night during long sleepless hours she lay in bed wondering what she had done to cause her husband to become so bitter, so suspicious, so unlike the man she thought she was marrying. Sometimes, as she waited for sleep, she remembered the words of the marriage ceremony. "For better, for worse," resounded through her mind.

"This is just a temporary thing," she promised herself. "Things will get better soon." And she redoubled her efforts to be the kind of wife Jonathan wanted and never to do anything that might cause him grief. She needed his love. She wanted his support. The loss of her privacy was a small price to pay if it would satisfy her Jonathan that she loved him.

Then Jonathan broached a new idea. Why didn't she resign her commission? Then she could stay at home all the time and be a proper wife to him, able to satisfy all his needs without him having to bottle them up waiting for her to come home from work. Nancy refused. She had worked long and hard to become a major. Someday she might become a lieutenant colonel. Her rank and her job brought her needed respect. Now that her marriage seemed to be falling apart, her work was even more important. At the hospital she could lose herself and forget her own worries while caring for others.

When she informed Jonathan that she felt she could not resign, he became furious. Glaring and shouting "Damn you!" he reached out and struck her a heavy blow to the eye, knocking her to the floor.

"Maybe that will teach you who is boss in this family!"

Nancy lay on the floor, holding her eye, and cried bitterly. "Oh Jonathan. How could you? How could you?"

He did not answer. The next day she went to work with a black eye. Even she found it unbelievable to try to explain it away by telling others she had walked into a door. Several of her coworkers looked at her with pity and sorrow.

A few days later, on her off day, while Jonathan was at work, Nancy received a phone call from one of her friends.

"Let's go shopping."

Nancy agreed.

They drove downtown and parked Nancy's car and then walked to Joske's By The Alamo. Nancy strolled through the aisles with her friend, not buying anything but just enjoying being out and having a relaxing time. That inner peace disappeared in an instant when she happened to see a man not far off who looked exactly like Jonathan, watching her. She got only a glimpse and then he disappeared, but she was sure it was Jonathan. Words tumbled through her mind.

"Why? Why? Doesn't he trust me? Of course not. So he sneaks around checking on me." Righteous anger was not a part of Nancy's personality. She concluded that "I will have to try harder to build his self-confidence. I must help him to trust me. I would never betray him. I have to help him know that."

As she drove home, Nancy pondered the event. Now she knew why Jonathan's salary had dropped so precipitously. Rather than going his rounds selling pharmaceutical products, he must have been spending his time following her.

After that first time, a darkness settled on Jonathan's soul. Having hit her once, it now seemed as if he took delight in hurting her. Nancy found it difficult to get through a day without being hit. More and more often she went to work with black eyes, facial and arm bruises. If others could see the rest of her body, they would find there multiple welts and bruises. Refusing to fight back, offering no resistance to Jonathan's temper, seemed to make him angrier. Now he began pulling off his belt when he became angry and yanking off her clothes and beating her with that leather strap.

Often the pain was so severe that she screamed in protest. She begged him to stop hurting her. Sometimes he did. At other moments her pleas seemed only to inflame him further. Even the neighbors in nearby houses noticed and heard her cries for help. Once as Jonathan kicked her in the kidneys and stomped on her legs as she lay on the floor, there came a pounding on the door.

"Police! Open up in there!"

By the time Jonathan admitted the two policemen, Nancy had slipped on a robe and was sitting in her recliner. She was able to talk coherently to the officers. She could not betray Jonathan. So she told her would-be saviors that she had fallen down the basement steps and had screamed for help until Jonathan heard her and came to her rescue. He had carried her upstairs, helped her get her robe on and put her in her chair. Yes. She would be alright. Jonathan concurred in her story. Shaking their heads in disbelief, the two police officers reluctantly left.

All was quiet in the house. Jonathan sat in his chair and glared at Nancy in her recliner. "Quick thinking, woman. Maybe you are learning who is boss here, after all."

Now Nancy found her days at work humiliating. The beatings caused her so much pain she often had to limp from room to room on her rounds at the hospital. Heavy makeup did not seem to disguise the bruises and black eyes on her face. She lied so regularly to her coworkers and supervisors that she began to run out of excuses. She couldn't continue to appear in public like this. Maybe it really might be better if she resigned her commission and stayed home.

Then came that unspeakable day when Jonathan lost control as she stood at the ironing board preparing her uniform for work. Screeching incoherently, he yanked the hot iron from her grasp, seized her around the wrist and held her bare arm while he branded her with the iron. The pain was so terrible she fainted. Later she called work and told them she was sick and would be unable to come in for a day or two. She carried that brand for the rest of her life.

She thought that was Jonathan at his very worst. He proved her wrong when during a later temper tantrum, he again seized one of her arms, stretched it out on the kitchen table so that it hung over the edge and bore down on it with his weight until the elbow became dislocated and both bones in her forearm broke. Then he picked her up, carried her into the bedroom and raped her. Her whimpers of pain seemed to inflame his passions. Only after he was spent did he allow her to seek medical help for her arm.

The examining physician at the hospital emergency room questioned her closely about how such a thing could have happened. Nancy had no answers, particularly when the doctor noticed the iron's brand on her other forearm. He said sternly that there were laws against such things. These injuries could not be self-induced or caused by an accident. They were clear signs of abuse. She needed to get away from whoever was doing this to her.

That rape was the day when she became pregnant. She acknowledged that condition to herself after she had missed two periods. She felt a tiny flare of hope. Perhaps being a father might change Jonathan back into the man he had been when they married. Caution about his reaction, caused Nancy to wait until her fourth month before she put a smile on her face and announced that she was pregnant. Jonathan's reaction was to slap her and ask "Who is the real father? Tell me!" Sulking, he ignored her completely for days. When he finally began to speak to her again it was only to make other insinuations about her secret sex life. Nancy felt betrayed. Alone. Abandoned. For the first time she started to wonder whether trying to save her marriage was worth all the pain it caused her.

Two months passed. Then one night Jonathan became enraged at something she said. Nancy was never sure, then or later, what it might have been. Rising from his chair, he pulled her from her recliner and threw her onto the floor. After kicking her in the kidneys, he rolled her over and kicked her in the belly with all his strength. She had never felt such pain. Two hours later she hemorrhaged and lost the baby.

When she was able, she called the hospital and arranged for a thirty-day leave. Totally demoralized and with her dreams of a happy marriage and becoming a mother gone forever, Nancy then took to her bed and lay there blindly staring at the walls. For two weeks she did not leave the bedroom except late at night to go to the kitchen and swallow a few bites of food. At least Jonathan had the decency to leave her alone and sleep in the guest bedroom.

She thought of the few times she had attended religious services in the time she had been in San Antonio. She had attended services at Cornerstone Church and had enjoyed the singing and the sermons by the fat preacher. Still sore, she waited until Jonathan was gone, got up and dressed gently, careful not to cause herself more hurt. Then she called a taxi and directed the driver to take her to Cornerstone Church.

He let her out at the church office. She hesitated for a long moment and then walked gingerly up the sidewalk and into a room where a secretary held sway.

"I want to see the preacher. Maybe he can help me find a place to hide. My husband has been abusing me. But he won't stand for me to leave him. If he finds me he will kill me. I am sure of it."

* * * * *

CHAPTER SEVEN

"I will extol thee, O Lord, for thou hast drawn me up and hast not let my foes rejoice over me. . . . I cried to thee for help . . . . Lord, thou hast brought up my soul from Sheol, restored me to life from among those gone down to the Pit."–Psalms XXX: 1-3.

As mankind recognized time, the spinning globe of earth turned until calendars proclaimed that the fourth month of the year 1970 was well over. It was homecoming time for two soldiers. Against all odds, almost miraculously, Captain Douglas MacArthur Andrews and Sergeant First Class Jan Lech Szigmond neared the end of their long journey south toward American lines. The trek had made their bodies lean, sinewy, stringy as braided rawhide. It was now second nature for them always to watch the distant horizon line for danger and to walk softly through the land under foot as if they trod a minefield. Enemy peoples were everywhere and there was but one chance of escaping. For the whole way they had to remain invisible. Doug was the one who told the story one dawn as they settled down under cover for a few hours respite.

"You know, Jan, we've been really lucky. The only other guy to do what we've done was an American Apache Indian named Masai. In the 1880s he jumped the Apache reservation in Arizona and for several years fought alongside Geronimo, one of the greatest guerilla fighters ever. Then he surrendered and was rounded up by the army for shipment to a prison maintained at Fort Taylor in St. Augustine, Florida. In Arizona the army put Masai onto a train headed for Florida. He was in a locked car and in chains. Then one night he disappeared from the train. He had somehow managed to break through the ceiling in one of the toilets and climb to the top of the train. Then he jumped off, probably somewhere in Mississippi or Alabama, a long ways from home. A few months later he showed up again at the reservation in Arizona. He had come home. And for that entire trip of over a thousand miles, including his crossing of the Mississippi River, not one soul ever seems to have seen him. We haven't had a thousand miles to cross, but we've been pretty successful being invisible."

"Yessir, Captain. Ve haf been lucky. Now yust a few miles to go." Not one to be terribly excited by history, Szigmond closed his eyes and drifted off to sleep.

Through three more nights they struggled on toward their objective. They moved at first dusk and continued on until false dawn lightened the sky before once again seeking cover. The 17th parallel came to seem to them much like the Holy Grail–ever sought for, never attained. Then one night they stumbled into a series of obstacles. Concertina wire. Dragon's teeth. Trip wires. Deadfalls. They stood at the near edge of these obstacles and wept. They had found the Demilitarized Zone.

On this side was death if they were caught. On the other side, just a kilometer or so away, was freedom. Yet now as they advanced they realized they had to be doubly careful. Now no one was their friend. This was a death zone. Anyone caught therein forfeited his right to life. Not only were they still targets for North Vietnamese Army soldiers as had been the case for all the months since their escape, but they were also fair game for any American soldiers lying in wait in listening posts and observation posts on the south side of the line. Men of U.S. units in I Corps, known as "Eye" Corps, were eternally watchful, prepared to waste any North Vietnamese who might try to sneak through the zone. They might well shoot first if they saw figures moving toward them and ask questions later. Much later. Too late for Doug and Jan, whose bodies would lie broken and bloody on land they had for so long sought.

They moved slowly, carefully checking for booby traps as they went. They were often slowed by seemingly endless stretches of razor wire. Their only choices were over, under or around. Bloody gashes testified to the mistakes they made. On through the endless hours of the night they crept forward. By dawn their nerves, always raw, were now stretched nearly past the breaking point. As the sky lightened, they reasoned that the greatest danger now lay to their front. They were far enough into the zone so that there was little likelihood of

114

their being spotted by any soldiers of the NVA. And so they began efforts to hail American watchers, repeatedly shouting as they walked. If they called attention to themselves in that way and walked upright and were seemingly harmless, they hoped that U.S. soldiers would come to meet them. If so they could then identify themselves. At last it came.

"Halt!"

"Halt, you ziphead shits."

"Hey guys," Andrews shouted. "Don't shoot. Don't shoot. We are Americans. We have escaped from prison in North Viet Nam. I'm Captain Douglas MacArthur Andrews. This is Sergeant First Class Jan Szigmond."

The sight of two armed and bearded skeletal men caused the hackles to rise on the three soldiers who challenged them.

"You got any identification?"

"No. All that was taken from us a long time ago by the NVA."

"Then squat on the ground, knees apart, hands behind your back while we check you out."

Two soldiers, M-16s at the ready, cautiously moved forward. They saw the rags the two men wore, the homemade sandals, the beards and long unkempt hair. They impounded the pistols, the AK-47 rifles, the homemade knife belonging to Jan. There was little else to check.

"You guys have dogtags?"

"Nope. They went AWOL along with all our other things."

"Well, there's nothing we can do except take you back to our company HQ."

It was a three man post. While one soldier remained in position, the other two prodded Doug and Jan along a narrow pathway into a clearing in which sat several tents and a supply trailer. They walked up to one tent and stopped.

"Here we are. You two wait right here!" The soldier turned his attention to the tent and shouted "Captain? Captain? You won't believe what we found up at the OP."

A young, healthy, tough-looking captain emerged from the canvas shelter, looked at Jan and Doug, and asked his men what the problem was. When informed that the two rag pickers had walked out of the zone a little after dawn, and claimed to have been prisoners of the NVA, the captain gawked. He stared at the two. He asked a few questions most of which were the same ones his men had asked earlier. Doug and Jan patiently answered him.

"You guys hungry?"

"Yes, Captain," Doug responded.

"Then come on. I'll see that you are fed."

He led the way to a mess tent, held back the flap, and the two escapees walked inside. The company commander spoke briefly with the mess sergeant who told the two to sit down. He would bring them food.

Scrambled eggs. Coffee. Bacon. Sausage. Grits. Reconstituted orange juice. Toast. Doug and Jan looked wonderingly at one another, grabbed their forks and dug into their piles of food, bolting down huge quantities. After a time, Jan laid down his fork and sat quietly for a moment. Then he leaped to his feet and ran outside where he vomited all he had eaten. Dry heaves beset him for several more minutes. Then he staggered back to the table and washed out his mouth with a drink of coffee.

"I guess it has been too long since we've eaten a rreal army meal, Captain."

He tentatively took another swallow of coffee. Doug fared better. He ate more slowly and consumed less and managed to hold it all down.

Doug looked at the company commander, still sitting at the table with them.

"What is the date, Captain?" he asked.

"Let's see. I've thirty-one days until DEROS, so this must be the last day of May."

"Tell me what year it is," Doug asked softly.

"You really have been out of it, haven't you? It's 1970."

116

"My God," said Doug. "I've been a prisoner since February 1967–three years and three months." Desperation was written on his face as he thought of those lost years of his life. Of the desperation. The frustration. The fear. The longing for Nancy West. The isolation of his cell. The pain inflicted on him. Yet despite all that, he and Jan had done what no one else had accomplished since America entered the conflict in Viet Nam. Held prisoners of the NVA they had escaped and made their way south across dangerous and treacherous miles to the safety of American lines.

"How goes the war? Are we winning?"

"Hell no. Ever since Tet 1968 we've been on a downward slide to hell in this fucking country."

"Tet?"

"Yeah. During Tet in 1968, a time during which both sides generally stood down so the Viets could celebrate their new year, the NVA and the VC attacked in every province and in most of the large cities. Rocketed Tan Son Nhut and the American embassy and the presidential palace. For a time they held forty-four provincial capitals. They held on in Hue for over a month. Executed about five thousand people there. Used bulldozers. Dug huge pits. Marched their prisoners into them and shot them. It was hell. Sure we finally beat them back but it took the starch out of the war effort. Now we're just holding on, waiting until we can find a way to pull out. And nobody wants to be the last GI killed in 'Nam!!"

Doug found it difficult to accept how much conditions had changed since the time of his capture. It was no wonder that no American units had ever come busting north to encircle his prison and free those held captive there. He scratched idly at the inflamed skin on his hands. His mind tumbled backward to a conversation he had with his friend Don Stoddard. Stoddard had for a time been his commander but on a combat assault had taken a round through the shoulder and had to be medevaced. At that point Lieutenant Colonel Jeremiah Barrett had made Doug commander of Alpha Company, 2nd Battalion, 11th Brigade (Separate), 23rd Division. It was not many days later when Stoddard showed up at his old company to talk to Andrews. Andrews chuckled at the sight of him.

"Yeah, Cornfodder," Stoddard scoffed. "But I'll be wearing this shoulder and arm cast for several weeks. Not to worry. I've been transferred to Brigade for limited duty."

As he listened, Doug scratched at his fingers until they bled. Don shook his head in sympathy. "That stuff must be giving you fits." Disgusted by what he had done, Doug rummaged in one of the drawers of his desk and pulled out a leather bootlace. He slipped his University of South Florida senior class ring off his left hand, threaded the leather thong through it and tied both ends of the thong together.

"How many times do I have to tell you? I thought West Pointers were supposed to have quick minds. It's Cornhusker, not Cornfodder. And yeah," he said, "Damn metal makes it worse. I must be allergic." He hung the thong about his neck.

"Got to get up to see the Battalion Surgeon and get some more medicine for this shit." He continued to rub at his hands as they talked.

Doug wondered whatever had happened to his ring. He had kept it around his neck for weeks. It had been there when Alpha Company assaulted Yen Song (3). When he regained consciousness in the VC jungle field hospital it was gone.

"Who," he wondered, "had made off with it?" He continued to scratch at the rash that had almost become a part of him. His thoughts were interrupted.

"What I have got to do with you two," the company commander said, "is to send you along to Battalion. They will want to hear your story there. So let's finish up here. I'll turn you over to our supply sergeant to get you fitted out in proper uniforms. Then I'll get you on the way."

At Battalion headquarters they were introduced to the commander by the company commander who had accompanied them there. Once again they were asked to tell their story and, as had been the case at company level, the battalion commander decided that they should be escorted back to the divisional TOC, the tactical operations center, or command post headquarters. A short jeep ride brought them to division as the sun began to drop toward the horizon in the west. Their first day of freedom was drawing to a close. The divisional commander, a major general, called a staff meeting after he had learned who his two visitors were and when his officers were assembled he had Doug and Jan introduce themselves and tell their story. When they finished, they were asked repeated questions, not only by the personnel officer, the operations officer, and the "old man" himself, but by every officer at the table. Their listeners kept marveling at their story. Their capture. Their treatment for wounds. Their imprisonment. Doug's repeated torture. Their escape preparations. Their long trek south to the DMZ. It was a nearly unbelievable epic. All the hardship and mistreatment had not broken the spirit of these two men. Sergeant First Class Jan Szigmond said it best, borrowing a phrase he had heard somewhere. "That which does not kill me makes me strronger."

Doug and Jan had now been on their feet more than twenty-four hours and it was beginning to tell on them. They swayed as they stood to answer questions. Their tongues slurred words. Their minds, already slowed by months of starvation rations and little rest, refused to function. Recognizing that they were near collapse, the general ended the staff meeting and turned Doug and Jan over to the division surgeon who, after a brief examination, ordered them both into his hospital.

The physicians at the hospital clustered around the two men when they were admitted. Everyone wanted to see and hear them. They ordered an immediate medical evaluation and a battery of tests for them. Doug suffered from loss of weight and malnutrition, stomach parasites, amoebic dysentery, fungal skin rot, from badly healed broken feet. His nose, broken so often during his times of torture, had healed in such a way that his breathing was affected. Some muscles had been torn. He had strained ligaments. His joints had been injured and would require medical care.

Nurses were horrified at the condition of Doug and Jan. They oversaw their baths and then dressed them in hospital gowns. Szigmond complained about his lack of modesty in his new clothing. The nurses smiled and said he would get used to them. He would be wearing them for a long time.

Those same ladies took scissors to their hair and tried to trim it into some semblance of a military cut. They were given fruit juice, a light meal, and tucked into beds. They were the first real beds that either had slept in for years. Szigmond was in his only for a moment when he rolled off onto the floor and vomited up his meal. A kindly nurse held him and gave him tiny sips of water. When he was safely back in bed, the two men looked at each other, smiled, and were asleep in seconds. Both of them marveled that they were going to sleep at night, instead of during the day, and that they had no need to hide from anyone. They were now just like normal people!

Yet unlike normal people, they came instantly alert at almost every sound made in the ward, and hospital wards are notoriously noisy. As they wakened time and again, their bodies pumped with adrenalin so that they were ready for fight or flight. The months of their southward trek had left their mark. After each start, it took them long minutes before they calmed enough to sleep again. In his fitful sleep Doug dreamed of bloody bodies and ghoulish, haunted faces of dead Vietnamese at Yen Song (3).

The physicians shook their heads as they cataloged Andrews' injuries and quickly sent Doug for a laboratory workup, including a complete blood count (CBC) and a chemistry series. Doug's primary physician showed up at his bedside with the results.

"Well, young fellow, I have some news for you. Your CBC shows a hemoglobin count of 8.7 and a hematocrit of 26." He smiled. "Hematocrit refers to the number of red blood cells in the blood. We don't normally talk about 'red blood cells' anymore." The physician chuckled. "Now, since we are more 'scientific' than we used to be we call them 'erythrocytes.' You can, of course, see how that is a much better term." Again he smiled. "When that count is reduced, we also know that the hemoglobin will likewise be impaired. Hemoglobin?

That refers to oxygen-carrying protein of the red blood cells that transports oxygen to the body tissues. When its low, oxygen delivery is impaired and this has adverse effects on all body processes, including healing. Furthermore, Captain, a low hemoglobin account can make a guy tired, fatigued, having no energy. Sounds a lot like you doesn't it?"

Doug winced. "Come on, Doc. Put that in language I can understand!"

"Well, CBC means a complete blood count. Its results tell me that basically you are moderately anemic, probably caused by your malnutrition both in prison and on your trip south. Nothing to worry about. Not bad enough to be concerned. You also have, however, an electrolyte imbalance. To help you, we are going to hook you up to an IV rack."

Shortly this was done. Glass bottles filled with 5% dextrose and multivitamin solutions dripped their contents into his body. He was also given lactated ringers solutions. The doctor told Doug that they were giving him the human equivalent of an "oil change and engine tune-up."

Technicians then typed and cross-matched Doug's blood after which, later, he received a transfusion of two units of whole blood. The nurse started an IV line by inserting a large #18 gauge intravenous needle into the bend of his elbow–his anticubital space. She said she was sorry if she hurt him. He laughed and said it was mild after what he had experienced in the north. In any case, he told her, it was nice to learn new words. The doctor, he said, had been teaching him the medical words describing his condition, like 'anticubital.' Later he was x-rayed from head to toe: a skull series, pictures of the long bones of his arms and legs. Other film revealed the secrets of his chest, his feet, and a KUB for his kidneys, ureters and bladder.

Other test results began to come back. X-rays showed a small hairline fracture of the frontal bone of the skull, probably caused by his guards kicking him. No treatment of this was felt to be necessary. Doug's chest x-ray showed a well healed bullet wound, for which again, no treatment was deemed necessary. Andrew's physician talked to him about his close call.

"By all rights, Doug, you should have died when you were shot in the chest. That guy was aiming at your heart! Instead, at four inches left of center, the bullet barely missed your stomach and spleen. It passed above both without touching either of them. You were lucky. You still suffered damage to your oblique muscles, your diaphragm, and your latissimus, in that order, before the bullet exited out through your back. On its way it hit and broke a rib. Luckily the bone fragments probably exited your body along with the bullet. And so you survived, young man." The physician shook his head and patted his patient on his shoulder. "May you always be so lucky!"

Doug's feet proved to be more of a challenge. X-rays showed several tarsal fractures on both feet. Doug's insistence on walking on them while confined to his cell following beatings caused them to heal in a distorted but functional manner. However the fracture lines were heavily calcified and the physician told Doug they would cause him to have arthritic symptoms the rest of his life.

Now the hospital staff turned their attention to Doug's other joints that had been so stressed during his sessions of torture. They found that his shoulders, while not fractured, had not healed properly due to their repeated dislocations during his times spent with Colonel Thien. Doug learned a new word. One of his physicians told him that the medical fraternity referred to such dislocations as "complete luxations."

Doug grinned.

"Give me some more words, Doc. Maybe I'll become a physician when I get back home."

His shoulder joints suffered from a severe range of motion limitation accompanied by severe pain. Awakening of a morning Doug regularly found his shoulders to be stiff and causing him agony. Yet he did not complain for he had dealt with such physical limitations all the way south on his trek with Sergeant Szigmond. His doctor patted him on the arm.

"O.K., Captain. Here's another medical term for you. We abbreviate 'range of motion' into 'ROM.' And your ROM problems dictate that we send you to physical therapy BID." He smiled. "BID means twice a day, and you will come to hate me for sending you for PT and you'll feel venemous toward everyone who works with you. But it is necessary. What you will feel will be far less painful than what was done to you in the past. But if you are ever going to get over what happened to you in that prison cell, it is something you will have to bear."

Doug referred to his PT sessions as a medically sanctioned form of torture. Some of it was pleasant enough, as when moist heat was applied to both shoulders, for up to thirty minutes but the subsequent strengthening and stretching exercises insisted on by the therapist were difficult for Doug to get through without letting the pain he felt show too much. The worst part was that when he finally finished his morning treatment, he now could look forward to a repeat of the same torture when the end of day drew near. Seeing how difficult those times were, his physician ordered pain and sleeping medicine for him. They helped.

Slowly Doug's shoulder ROM improved and the associated aches and pains lessened. Moist heat applied to his spine helped correct the damage done there. Leg stretches proved helpful. Slowly his blood work also returned to normal. His skin rash disappeared. His badly broken nose was surgically reduced and then the physicians performed a rhinoplasty–cosmetic nose repair–to improve the distorted and misshapen appearance of Doug's face and to allow him better airflow. The day following the operation on his nose, Szigmond looked at him and smiled.

"Captain? You haf a rainbow on your face. Blue. Brown. Black. Yellow. Purple."

Doug was dewormed with an antihelminthic medication and without those parasites his stomach functioned again properly for the first time in a long while. Good food and IV solutions remedied his malnutrition. Yet it all took so very long at a time when Doug was anxious to return home and see his loved ones.

He learned why days spent in a hospital were called "slow time." He was there for weeks each day of which seemed like an eternity. He discovered how monotonous hospital routine became, and it irked him when he realized that it was for the convenience of the staff rather than for the comfort of the patient. Yet slowly his body healed. But what about his mind and the vivid flashbacks he suffered both while asleep and awake? The hospital psychiatrist told him that it might be a very long time before the horrors his mind retained began to dissipate.

Jan Szigmond was more fortunate and he did not need much in the way of medical intervention. His freedom to move about in the prison and his ability to provide himself with extra food unbeknownst to the guards now stood him in good stead. His blood work showed only very mild abnormalities in addition to malnutrition and loss of weight. These were easily corrected by proper nutrition, three squares plus snacks daily. His chest X-ray revealed only a mild, bilateral lower lobe infiltrate. All those weeks of sleeping in the open, often while wet, nearly always cold had seemingly given him only a low grade pneumonia. As treatment he was given ten days of antibiotics and breathing treatments, administered by a respiratory therapist who met with him twice daily.

The physicians at first were concerned because Szigmond had vomited his food, so they checked his stools and vomitus for occult, or hidden, blood. They were checking for a gastrointestinal ulcer but results were negative. A flat plate X-ray of Jan's abdomen ruled out any bowel obstruction as a cause for his vomiting, so the physicians told him his vomiting most likely was caused by a simple factor–he was eating too fast after having been starving for so long.

A physician stopped by Jan's bed to give him the good news that nothing had been found. "As medical people, Sergeant, we have to check everything. Otherwise we would be derelict in our duties. And anyway, there's an old hospital saying that when doctors hear hoof beats they look for zebras." He laughed heartily and moved on to his next patient.

Prior to his capture Szigmond, six feet tall, had weighed one hundred and seventy pounds. When admitted to the hospital, he found he had lost fifty pounds in captivity. The same was true for his partner. Doug was six feet one inch and on the day of the Yen Song (3) attack, he weighed one hundred and eighty. While imprisoned his weight dropped to one hundred and fifteen pounds.

Both men steadily improved, Jan did so quickly, Doug managed to regain his strength slowly. They both marveled in life without pain, in improved strength, and in their weight gain.

The three-star commander of Eye Corps came calling and spoke with Doug and Jan as they lay on their beds. He was as impressed by their story as had been those of lesser rank and lower commands. He tried to answer questions posed to him by Doug.

"Yes, Captain. Your old outfit, 11th Brigade, 23rd Division, is still operational and located in II Corps. Its had a couple of commanders since you were captured. Moore was yours, wasn't he? I don't know where Vernon Moore is now. He was nicknamed 'Savage.'" The general chuckled. "I do know that he got his brigadier's star after a successful follow up to that fucked up operation when you were captured. I've heard that he is now in some stateside command, but don't know which one. I guess I could find out if it is important to you."

"No sir. It's o.k. Thanks anyway. Do you know about my battalion commander, Jeremiah Barrett?"

"Yes, son. He was killed in action about the same time as Moore's successful operation against the VC in the Pinko Peninsula. Damn shame."

"Sir, is there any chance you might ever have heard of a man who was my best friend, a guy who back then held the rank of Major, an officer named Donald Stoddard?"

"No, Captain. I don't usually keep track of majors unless they work directly for me."

Later the general relaxed in the divisional commander's office at the TOC, ruminating on the experiences of the two men and the absolute dedication they had both exhibited in order to make that dramatic escape.

"We need to do something for those two men," spoke the Eye Corps commander. "Let's see. They both need to be given high awards. Let's go for the best. Sergeant Szigmond deserves a silver star. Captain Andrews might well be in line for a Medal of Honor. Tell you what. You put them in for those awards. You put them in and I'll sign off on them. We can take care of Szigmond's medal right here, in house. We can get Andrews' award started here and then forward it to proper authority with our strongest recommendations that it be awarded. Does that sound like a plan?"

The divisional commander nodded in agreement, already thinking how he should word the recommendations.

* * * * *

"Yes, Nurse. The number is 308-946-2283." She carefully dialed and then handed the phone to Major Douglas MacArthur Andrews. Doug put the handset to his ear and listened with great apprehension as the electronic synapses and relays clicked away the thousands of miles between Viet Nam and his quiet home town of Central City, Nebraska.

He could hear the phone ring. Once. Twice. Three times. Then he heard the voice of his beloved mother.

"Hello?"

"Hi, mom. It's Doug. I love you."

He heard a sudden intake of breath and then a sob.

"My son is dead. I buried him. This is cruel. Who is this?"

"No, mom, it's really me. I was captured and held prisoner in North Viet Nam. Another man and I escaped. We just got back to American lines a few days ago. It's really me. I love you. Oh, mom, I love you very much. I'm alive!"

He heard his mother shout. "Chalmers, Laura. Get on the phone. There is some man talking to me who claims he is Doug."

His father's voice came through clearly. "Who is this?"

Another extension clicked and Laura spoke. "Doug? Are you really alive?

126

"There are laws against this kind of thing, mister. Now get off the phone and don't bother us again. Do you hear me?" His father sounded wrathful.

Doug struggled for breath, his chest constricted and his throat swollen with emotion. "Mom, dad, Laura? It's really me. Believe me. We live on north 17th Avenue. I went to school at the University of South Florida. You all came down for my ROTC commissioning. Ezekiel Andrews was my great grandfather. His wife died young. Her name was Anne Blakely. My grandfather was Joshua. He married Wanda Bradley. Dad, during the war you trained at Camp Blanding in Florida and then shipped out to Europe to serve with the 28th Division and in the Huertgen Forest you were shot through one of your lungs. Mom? Your maiden name was Anise. Charlotte Anise. No stranger would know these things. It's me. Doug. I'm alive."

His mother and Laura began to sob. Chalmers spoke brokenly into the phone. "Then who did we bury?"

"I don't know, Dad. I don't know."

"When his body was recovered, he had your class ring in his pocket. It was crushed. I had it repaired and haven't taken it off my finger since I got it back from the jewelry store. Who was he?"

"I don't know, Dad. I was allergic to the metal. I took it off and hung it around my neck. The leather string must have broken and it fell on the ground there at Yen Song (3). That's the only explanation I have."

"My God, son. You don't know how often I have prayed for this. But if you didn't die, then what happened to you?"

His mother's voice broke in. "Dougie, I love you so much. So very much."

His father's voice overrode hers.

"What happened to you, Doug?"

"I guess we'll both have to live with chest wounds, Dad. I was on an assault of a little Vietnamese hamlet . . . ."

"Yes, I know. We were told. We were also told that everyone was massacred by the Vietnamese. Including you. That was over three years ago. Now you turn up. What happened? Why did you live when all the others died?"

"Dad, do you know what a *chieu hoi* is?"

"No. Tell me."

"A *chieu hoi* is an enemy soldier, usually VC, who surrenders to the government, turns in his weapon, and is forgiven for his rebellion. Many then go on to become interpreters and scouts for American units. Our *chieu hoi* at 2nd Battalion was a traitor. He's the one who led the enemy troops to our location."

Doug knew he should have died that day. To have survived was somehow almost wrong and he felt great guilt that only he among so many could still walk the earth. He slowly continued his explanation.

"I tried to play dead, but the *chieu hoi* found me and realized I was faking it. So he shot me. I did almost die. Then someone or other decided I might be more use alive than dead, so they took me to a VC field hospital where some half trained physician with no equipment patched me up. When I was well enough to travel, I was taken north and put in a prison there. I found out that my old platoon sergeant was also there. We helped each other."

Doug skipped over the harshness of life in prison and the torture to which he had been repeatedly subjected. There was no way he could make his family understand and there was no point in burdening them with that knowledge.

"So we escaped and made our way south. And Dad," Doug said, "here I am. Alive and almost well and aching to see all of you. I'll be home just as soon as they discharge me from this hospital. Oh yes, and by the way, the army gave me credit in rank for the time I was a POW and so I was just promoted to major."

The conversation went on accompanied by weeping, sounds of joy, and exclamations of happiness as the full realization sunk into the Andrews' minds that their son and brother was really there, that in time he would come home to them. Then Doug could no longer hold back the question that had haunted him for so long.

"How's Nancy? Tell me about her."

128

There was an awkward and embarrassing pause. Then all three of the Andrews' family began to speak at once. After much shushing, Charlotte gave an explanation.

"We kept in close contact with her for over a year, Doug. She came to your funeral. She and Laura became good friends. Then, after a time, she married a pharmaceutical salesman, Jonathan Diedrich. They live in San Antonio and Nancy, who is now also a major, is assigned to Brooke Army Medical Center. We got a letter from her not long ago that she is going to have a baby. We haven't heard since."

Doug was crushed under the weight of those words. He had dreamed about her for years. He saw her face in his dreams. Thoughts of her kept him sane as he lay nearly insensate in his cell after torture sessions. Her memory strengthened him during those dark hours. He had sworn to free himself so he could see her again. Hold her in his arms. Make love to her. Marry her. And now this. He was so sunken into a fugue by this news that after a few more sentences he ended the phone conversation with a whispered "I love all of you." He put the phone back in its cradle, sat down on his bed, toppled over and continually rubbed his eyes as silent and bitter tears flooded from them.

* * * * *

"How do my new stripes look, Capta . . . uhh, Majorr?"

"They look good on you Jan!" He paused. "Did you know that division and corps have put me in for a Medal of Honor? They've got you down for a Silver Star."

Jan nodded. He was aware of the awards.

"I am not going to accept it, even if it is approved. I don't deserve one. The MOH is for heroism and I am no hero. I hid from the enemy while my men died. I let myself be captured. I confessed that I was a pirate and that the U.S. was an aggressor nation. All I really did was escape and I couldn't have done that without you. You're the one who deserves the MOH, Jan. Certainly not me. What you did, what you accomplished, is worth more than a silver star. And I won't take it, even if it approved.

129

"Nonsense, Majorr. You have set an example for otherrs. You have lived herroically. I know. I vas therre! If you won't accept it for yourrself, accept it for otherrs and on their behalf. Accept it for all those who have died herre in Wiet Nam. Don't be asshole, Major!"

Doug's lips twitched momentarily in a smile at the tone used by Master Sergeant Jan Szigmond and then disappeared as the void in his chest caused by the loss of Nancy West pushed all humor from him

* * * * *.

Doug was surprised at the sheer size of the man with the hamlike hands and long, creased face, set off by two jug ears. His thin hair was swept back , plastered against his skull. He wore an expensive suit and white, French cuffed shirt with diamond cuff links. On his lapel ostentatiously sat his Silver Star, awarded him in 1942 by General Douglas MacArthur himself in recognition of his having ridden in a bomber that had been attacked by Japanese airplanes before it could return to its base in Australia. Ever since his return to the House of Representatives and then the Senate and, finally, to the Presidency itself, Lyndon Johnson proudly displayed his hero's gong and wore it on every possible occasion. Now he stood quietly, patiently, behind the podium waiting for the final strains of martial music by the Marine Band to fade away.

Major Douglas MacArthur Andrews and Master Sergeant Jan Lech Szigmond stood at attention six paces in front of the President of the United States. Behind them, in folding chairs placed on the lawn of the rose garden sat assembled dignitaries including the Chief of Staff of the Army and the Secretary of Defense. None of them mattered to Andrews. It was the proud members of his family that counted. He knew that Laura and his mom would be holding handkerchiefs to their eyes and that his dad would be looking on with a smug smile on his face. Proud and happy, they would be rejoicing that their son and brother was about to receive the nation's highest decoration from the President himself.

Homecoming had been joyous, full of smiles and touches and hugs, late night conversations and tears. It was marred only by his inability to locate Nancy Diedrich (he still felt revulsion when he thought of her married name) to let her know that he was alive and almost well. BAMC did not know where she was, only that she had taken indefinite leave. Her telephone had been discontinued. The mortgage company told him that the Diedrichs had missed several house payments and so their home had been repossessed. No one had come forward to protest that action. Inquiries of their neighbors were no more fruitful. Nancy was a very sweet woman who must have been very clumsy for she often bore bruises from falling.

Jonathan was no longer employed by the pharmaceutical firm and no one there knew his whereabouts. They could only advise that during his last months of employment his work had shown a dramatic down turn. Doug did not know where to look next.

A chaplain stepped forward to offer an invocation. Chaplain (Colonel) Paul Eastley. Doug had discovered that his friend was now commandant of the U.S. Army Chaplain Center and School and had asked him to participate in the White House ceremony. Eastley joyously accepted and when the two met they held their hug for long minutes. Now he was at the podium to offer his prayer.

Doug admired the chaplain, only a few years older than he and a fellow Central Citian. As a boy Paul had scooped snow from the sidewalks of the Andrews' home during World War II when Chalmers was in the army and his dad, feeble old Josh Andrews, was still alive. Now a mature man, he stood resplendent in his dress blue uniform with its black facings and gold trim on jacket and sleeves and with gold stripes running down the seam of his trousers. On his chest above his left pocket he wore a bank of five ranks of medals including the Silver Star and two Purple Hearts. Above the ribbons the Combat Infantryman's Badge was affixed, awarded to him for extraordinary bravery during combat while he was with Doug Andrews' platoon. Also fastened to his blouse were Jump Wings and on his shoulder he wore the Ranger tab. He was now a man of stature and importance and yet had gladly agreed to attend the rose garden ceremony.

Chaplain (Colonel) Paul Eastley asked the audience to bow their heads. After a moment of silence, he began.

"Almighty God, we are assembled here to honor two soldiers who have brought great credit upon themselves, the Army, and this nation. Thou art the Lord of history and through thy power men have won liberty. By thy justice our fathers beheld the vision of a righteous nation. By thy will, over the decades, many have laid down their lives as a sacrifice to this country. We are mindful of our heritage, not of our own deserving but by thy providence. Help us to be worthy to stand in this place in the time allotted to us, and with steadfast courage and unwavering hope fulfill the tasks which are ours."

The chaplain paused a moment, and then went on.

"Deliver us of this conflict in Viet Nam which has stolen the lives of so many of our young men and brought others broken in mind and body back to these shores. Help our leaders understand now, before another day shall pass, the waste and tragedy of this war. May it end, once and for all, and may your Name be glorified, now and forevermore. In the Name of Jesus Christ, your beloved Son. Amen."

Eastley opened his eyes, replaced his headgear, smartly saluted Doug and Jan, and stepped back from the podium. As he did so he glanced at the President and saw the bleak look with which Mr. Johnson regarded him. "Good," he thought to himself. "He listened to my prayer." And he sent a petition skyward. "May he not only hear but act on it now."

President Johnson gripped the edges of the podium as a slow smile brightened his face. "Major Andrews . . . Master Sergeant Szigmond, please come forward." The two men did so, moving three paces nearer and then once again assuming the position of attention.

"Master Sergeant, it gives me great pleasure to award you the Silver Star . . . a decoration which I also hold, given to you in recognition of your valor, your dedication to duty, and your devotion to this country. You and your major are singular. No other American has done what the two of you achieved. Your award will now be pinned on you by the Secretary of Defense." He nodded and that official stepped forward and opened the box proferred to him by the

President in which lay the Silver Star. He pinned it on Szigmond's jacket, saluted him, and then stepped back into place.

"Major Andrews, your division and corps commanders have seen fit to recommend you for this nation's highest award for valor. There are but few in any generation who qualify for this Medal of Honor. I speak truly when I say I would rather wear this medal than to be President of the United States." He took the starred ribbon from which hung the sacred pendant and placed it around Doug's neck. Then Mr. Johnson stepped back and saluted the major as the band once again began playing.

* * * * *

Major Douglas MacArthur Andrews was assigned to the Pentagon while Szigmond was sent to serve as the First Sergeant of an infantry unit in Washington State. Their leave-taking of one another was fervent for they had known and worked together with the other for over four years. They had shared combat. They suffered together in imprisonment. Together they had beaten the odds and escaped. Now, at long last, the Army system was sending them in separate directions. They gripped hands tightly. They hugged and pounded one another on the back. Then Szigmond stepped back and said something to the major that Doug had never expected to hear. "Zank you forr being my friend."

Andrews moved into two rooms at the Military Towers, a high rise motel used primarily by men and women assigned to the Pentagon. It was convenient, located on a major bus route that could take him to work and then deposit him back at his rooms in the afternoon. There was also a nearby cafeteria to which he could walk to take his meals, and the food there was palatable.

During duty hours he was faced with seemingly endless interrogation about his imprisonment and his time as a POW. There was always one more question to be answered, one more report to write out. And so passed the days. The nights became more restful as the dreams about Yen Song (3) began to pass into hidden recesses of his mind.

Then came a great unpleasantness. One day as Doug sat at his desk in his minuscule cubicle, a general walked in. "Don't fuckin' get up, Major. Just stopped by to see how the fuck you're doing." It was Brigadier General Vernon "Savage" Moore, and he had not just "happened" to drop by. He had traveled across many state lines to get there.

Their meeting was short. There were no pleasantries. Moore lit a cigar, sat down and leaned back. "Major, you and I are the only ones alive who know what happened at that fuck-up at Yen Song (3). Your troops are dead. Your battalion commander is dead. The pilot that took me over the area is dead. Only you and me. You might someday be tempted to explain to someone that part of the reason for that massacre was the order I gave to Barrett to "take care of" the inhabitants. And goddamit, you'd be right. But I don't intend to have any marks on my record. I want a second star, and a third. Maybe even a fourth before I retire. Anyway, part of it–maybe even the biggest part--was your own stupidity in not controlling your men. Too bad the gooks didn't kill you. Then I'd be the only one who knows and I goddam well don't plan on ever tellin' anyone. Now with you back in circulation, I got another fly in my ointment. You've been warned. Keep your goddam mouth shut. I won't ever tell you again."

Without another word, Moore got to his feet and left. During the entire episode Doug had not said a word, simply listening in amazement to this war dog.

* * * * *

It was a hot July afternoon in 1970 and Chalmers, alone in his home study, sat in his leather chair facing his desk while staring into space. His mind churned through the events of the past weeks. His son had been resurrected as surely as Lazarus had walked from the grave. He remembered the prayer he had offered at the funeral. His son's body had been identified because of the ring. "Oh Lord," he had said, "what if Doug gave his ring to someone else? What if he lost it and someone else found it? Then he might be alive somewhere as a prisoner and the body in that casket might belong to someone else. If only he'd come back to me." And even as he prayed he knew that his

134

words would rise no higher than the ceiling of the church in which he sat. But they had. And now his son had returned. The only thing that marred Doug's days, and consequently also the days of Chalmers and Charlotte, was the mystery of the whereabouts of Nancy Diedrichs.

The phone rang. Chalmers answered. "Hello?"

"Is this Mr. Andrews?" a soft voice asked.

"Yes it is. Who is this?"

"Mr. Andrews, this is Nancy West. I am so afraid. I have been hiding from Jonathan for weeks in this woman's shelter here in San Antonio. Oh Mr. Andrews. He was so cruel. He beat me. He made me lose my baby. He would have killed me, and so I ran. Now I am afraid he is going to find me. Yesterday the matron said that a man had been here asking questions about me. Can you help me? I know I have no right to ask, but I have no one else to turn to."

"Nancy, where are you now? Give me an address and I'll be there tomorrow. And don't go outside for any reason whatsoever. Tell those in charge what I look like and to admit me when I call. And Nancy? Doug's alive! He was wounded and became a POW and just recently managed to escape. He has looked everywhere for you. Thank you for reaching out. He loves you still and so do we all. I will see you tomorrow."

* * * * *

CHAPTER EIGHT

"I have fought a good fight, I have finished my course, I have kept the faith: Henceforth there is laid up for me a crown of righteousness, which the Lord, the righteous judge, shall give me at that day . . . ."–II Timothy IV: 8.

A car backfired out in the street. Nancy jumped, startled for a moment by the sudden noise.

"Chalmers, I wonder if I will ever stop being afraid of Jonathan? Jumping at every sound?"

It was early in the morning two days after Chalmers had received her call. He had made a quick trip to San Antonio, collected her from the woman's shelter after she had a chance to pack a few things. Then it was off to the airport. Now she was safe with the Andrews family in Central City. Charlotte and Laura poured out their love when she arrived. When they saw Nancy walk in the door of their home, they shrieked and laughed and cried and hugged almost without let. At this moment, the next morning, they were still in bed and Nancy and Chalmers sat in the breakfast nook drinking coffee.

"Yes, Nancy, I think the time will come when you will no longer be afraid of him. Maybe that's not too far into the future. In the meantime I have asked for a restraining order on him and I have filed felony battery charges against him. If we can locate him, he will have a lot to answer for. And just so you know, I have retained a private detective to try to locate him." He smiled. "Some time today I will also introduce you to a young man who is moving in with us. No. No. I am not trying to 'fix you up.' I am bringing him here to act as a bodyguard for you for a few weeks, just until we can locate Jonathan. He's ex-Army Special Forces, Ranger qualified, and holds a ninth degree black belt in some oriental fighting method. Judo or Tai Quan Do or Karate or some such. He will also be carrying a weapon. I don't really think Jonathan is going to want to meet him!"

Nancy shivered. She looked so helpless that Chalmers reached out and covered her hand with his. He stared. Ridges of scar tissue had formed around her eyes, caused by her husband's blows. One ear was a cauliflower shape, much as an old boxer would have. Yet she was still beautiful and he hoped things worked out so that she could become his daughter-in-law.

"Don't be frightened, darling. I will see to it that no one hurts you, ever again. Now we need to get on the telephone over there and call Doug and tell him what has happened."

"Chalmers, I don't want him to see me. I am so afraid. I have looked at myself in the mirror. I know I look awful."

"Honey, you are beautiful. And he will love you as he always has. I suspect that when he found out that you were married, he still prayed that one day things might work out for you and him. Now. Be brave. I am going to dial his number and, hopefully, get him before he leaves for the Pentagon."

He picked up the receiver, held it between his ear and hunched shoulder and dialed 202-695-5206. He could hear it begin to ring. Then his son's voice came on the line.

"Hello. This is Major Andrews. May I help you?"

"Hi Doug, it's Dad."

"Dad! Nice surprise. What got you out of bed so early?"

"I have a surprise for you, son. I have someone here with me that I think you will want to talk to. Wait . . ." He handed the phone to Nancy.

She took it reluctantly, held it to her ear, sighed, and started to speak but no words came out. She tried again.

Douglas MacArthur Andrews heard a tremulous female voice, saying "Doug? Doug. We thought you were dead. I'm sorry. I didn't mean to hurt you. There was never a day that I didn't think of you when I waked up. You were in my thoughts as I laid down to sleep. But you were dead and so I married Jonathan. He seemed so nice, but he turned into a monster. He hurt me and made me lose my baby. Oh Doug, I love you so! Please forgive me."

"Nancy? Oh my God, is that you? Why are you with my folks? I love you too, honey, with all my heart. I"ll never stop loving you.

They talked for an hour. They hung up the phones. Nancy cried when his voice was gone even as Doug headed for the office to seek a thirty day emergency leave.

The next day, using one of the Andrews' cars, Nancy and her bodyguard drove to Omaha to pick Doug up from his flight home. She waited just inside the last gate area at the end of the long hallway of the low slung Eppley Airfield and when Doug's flight was announced she went to wait with others just outside the terminal, standing on the tarmac near where planes landed and taxied up to unload.. The arriving passengers walked down the aluminum steps from the plane and moved toward the arrival gate. Nancy peered carefully at each man, heart throbbing, waiting for the right one to reach her. Then she was in his arms, embraced in a hug that she never wanted to end. Both sobbed. She looked at him. He was tall and straight, as she remembered. His weight was about right. Only his nose was different, struck and broken too many times by his tormenters before his escape. It had healed badly and was askew to the left and flatter than she remembered. She pulled his head down to her lips and kissed his nose. "My darling," she murmured, "I love you with all my heart."

"And I love you." He paused. Then he said, "Let's go home, Nancy."

* * * * *

Months earlier, not long after Doug's escape and at about the time President Johnson awarded him the Medal of Honor, one of his old friends telephoned him. Don Stoddard. Now Lieutenant Colonel Stoddard. They spoke a few words and reminisced for a moment or two. Then Don said goodbye. Doug looked at the receiver he still held in his hand and wondered why his friend had seemed so cold. They had shared a friendly rivalry since the first day of their training at the Infantry Officer Basic course at Fort Benning when they were both brand new second lieutenants. They amused themselves by baiting one another as the days stretched into months during which time they had gone on to the Advanced course, to jump school, to Ranger training.

Stoddard was the only son of a school superintendent in Pulaski, New York. His one goal in life, adopted by the time he was ten, was to serve as an officer in the Army. Upon his graduation from high school he received a congressional appointment to the United States Military Academy at West Point. Slender, tough, as muscled as a braided whip, there was little he could not do easily. He graduated thirty-fifth in the Class of 1964. His education did not make him an intellectual. He did not even enjoy reading a book. But the teaching and discipline of West Point implanted in him forever the desire to serve the military and his country to the best of his ability. He was enthralled when he sat in the auditorium on 12 May 1962 and listened to the great and very elderly General Douglas MacArthur offer his thoughts on the occasion of his accepting the Thayer Award. Now eighty-two, MacArthur's eloquence resonated within Stoddard's soul as he listened to the general speak of "This beloved land of culture and ancient descent." He recalled "gaunt, ghastly men," who gave their lives for their country and recalled "twenty campaigns, on a hundred battlefields, around a thousand campfires." The General had, he said, listened to 'the mournful mutter of musketry' and had seen his soldiers staggering "on many a weary march from dripping dusk to drizzling dawn."

MacArthur's days of old, he said, "have vanished–tone and tints." His words, however, were not meant solely to recall the past but to point to the future for the cadets who listened that day. He abjured them to walk justly and perform faithfully. "Duty, Honor, Country–these three hallowed words reverently dictate what you want to be, what you can be, what you will be." He said that "they build your basic character. . . . the very obsession of your public service must be Duty, Honor, Country." Were those who listened to fail in that task, "a million ghosts in olive drab, in brown khaki, in blue and gray, would rise from their white crosses thundering Duty, Honor, Country." In closing, this old soldier told the young men who sat there absorbed that his "last thoughts will be of the Corps and the Corps and the Corps."

Stoddard stood in the midst of his clapping fellows with tears running down his face. He was stirred far beyond anything that had ever gone before. He would never forget. And he would always be faithful, he promised himself, to Duty, to Honor, to Country.

Two years later, still able to quote many of MacArthur's words, Don was commissioned a second lieutenant of Infantry. In his initial officer's training, Stoddard enjoyed meeting and becoming friends with Douglas MacArthur Andrews. It was, he thought, ironic that his hero and his friend both bore the same name. They were classmates through all their training days. They were then sent to the same first assignment, teaching trainees at Fort Lewis in Washington State.

Together they went to Viet Nam where both were assigned to the 23rd Division, 11th Brigade. Don served on Brigade staff, Doug went to 2nd Battalion as a platoon leader. They saw one another occasionally. Then for a time, until he was wounded, Stoddard, who had been promoted faster than Doug and who was now a captain, served as Doug's company commander.

Stoddard had been a fun loving young man, but the years had not only aged him but had stripped him of his sense of humor. There was too much sadness in life, too much bloodshed and horror, for anyone to crack a joke or feel light hearted. Frown lines embedded themselves on his face. He was a formidable man and those who worked for him walked carefully. He was never unjust or biased, but when he was displeased with performance he let the miscreant know it with absolute clarity.

Now, with Doug having returned from the dead, Stoddard was faced with a quandary. He was glad his old friend had not died but his joy was dampened by his memories. He recollected all too well his long talk with Doug's battalion commander, Lieutenant Colonel Jeremiah Barrett, following the massacre at Yen Song (3) and the subsequent slaughter of the American soldiers there. Barrett had told him how the brigade commander, "Savage" Moore had exulted that it was a good thing the GIs had died, for now no one would ever know how they had butchered the inhabitants of the tiny hamlet. Barrett and Moore knew. Their pilot knew. He had flown the brigade commander's helicopter over the scene and they had watched the butchery.

Stoddard remembered the days that followed. The pilot's helicopter mysteriously blew up out over the South China Sea. Lieutenant Colonel Jeremiah Barrett was shot by a sniper. Now only Moore knew. Not quite so. Major Donald Stoddard also knew. He had accidentally encountered Barrett one evening not long after the massacre. The man was drunk and clung to Stoddard's shoulder as Don took him to the officer's club for coffee to help him sober up. Instead Barrett ordered a double whiskey and then another and another. He began to ramble, probably no longer aware even of who it was he sat with.

"God," he had slurred. "The blood. I've never seen anything like it. At least twenty-nine bodies in that ditch. All machined gunned. Even women and children. Some were still moving. I'll never get over it." He signaled for still another double whiskey.

"Colonel, why don't you tell me all about it. What happened? Tell me from start to finish. Maybe you'll feel better just by talking to someone."

Barrett had done so. Afterwards, Don had gone to his office and written up in some detail as many things as he could recall that the increasingly incoherent Barrett had told him. A massacre. And then a second massacre. Americans against the inhabitants of a Vietnamese hamlet. Then Vietnamese troopers against the GIs. No survivors. Poor damn lost Doug and all the others. Stoddard sighed. What was his responsibility now that he knew this story?

Directives were clear. Anyone with knowledge of violations of the USMACV rules of engagement were required to report them to higher headquarters. But Moore at Brigade was higher headquarters and, if Barrett spoke accurately, Moore intended to bury the entire episode. That left Division. His duty lay in reporting to the inspector general and commanding officer there.

Would that bring Doug back? Such a report would not only smear his good friend's name, but it would smear the name of every

U.S. soldier at Yen Song (3) that day. It would also bring suffering to Doug's family, to the families of all those he commanded and who had died that day. He remembered a phrase from one of Chaplain (Major) Paul Eastley's scripture readings he had listened to one Sunday. "Let the dead bury the dead."

Stoddard rose from his desk, shoving his notes into a brown manila envelope. Calling out to two men also working late there in the office, he sealed the brown flap, asking them to sign their names and the date across the overlap of envelope and flap. Below their names he signed his own name and again wrote the date. Opening his file cabinet, he pulled a drawer out to its furthest extension and carefully placed the envelope at the rear. He grimaced as he slammed the drawer shut. And that should have been that.

When Captain Stoddard DEROSed back to the States, he packed that envelope with his other things and took it home with him. His next assignment was to serve on staff at Fort MacPherson, Georgia. He had no plans for that envelope; he simply did not want to leave it behind where it might be found by others. It was, after all, his secret. Even as he did so, he felt a ghostly finger pointing at him and heard the voice of General MacArthur intoning those three words: Duty, Honor, Country.

The episode should have died there. That was truly the end of it. Except that Douglas Andrews rose from the dead and once more walked the land of the living. He now wore the Medal of Honor above the Silver Star that Colonel "Savage" Moore had "posthumously" awarded him. He was a hero, respected, admired, a role model for younger officers. Army Times had published a long feature on the escape of Andrews and Szigmond. They had been featured in dozens of newspapers and had appeared on the covers of both Life and Time. Doug had been offered book contracts, with advances high enough to make him a rich man. There was even talk of making a movie. Yet, Stoddard reluctantly thought, Andrews was a butcher of women and children, of the old and the unarmed, of the innocent and the harmless. What about them? Then there was Major General "Savage" Moore, only a colonel and brigade commander at the time, who had covered his tracks and been handsomely promoted by his government. Should he profit from such a misdeed? Duty. Honor. Country. He opened the old envelope and once again assessed its contents.

If he acted, Doug would face additional grief after he had already suffered more than anyone should ever have to endure. He was back home and thinking of picking up the threads of his life once more. The words of Don's notes haunted him. What should he do? He could destroy his statement and keep mum about it for the remainder of his life, or he could notify proper authority. Doug was his friend and fellow comrade. Yet a crime had been committed at Yen Song (3) and the crime should be investigated.

In any case, exactly what was Doug guilty of except having been there? It was a platoon of his company that had destroyed the hamlet. A commander is always held responsible for the misdeeds of those below him. What should he do?

* * * * *

Joy had come to the Andrews' home in full measure, heaped up and running over. The walls of the house resonated with the buzz of conversations, with laughter, with happiness not found therein since Doug had been reported killed in action three years earlier. Charlotte discovered that she needed no reason, save love, to give her son still another hug. Chalmers looked forward daily to the wide ranging conversations he had with Doug. Laura listened to them, eyes glistening with pride, lips pursed in smiles.

The greatest happiness belonged to Doug and Nancy. They could not get enough of touching one another, of clinging tightly to each other, of endless talking and murmuring, of smiles and caresses. They both avoided discussing the hard times of their past save that Doug told her how hard life in prison had been and how much he owed to Sergeant First Class Jan Szigmond. In turn Nancy told only that Jonathan had changed from the man she had married into a being she could no longer recognize. She reached out to her lover and told him how his new nose made him look debonair and dashing. He touched the iron's brand on her arm and gathered her once more into still another embrace.

144

Shadowing Nancy, but always carefully staying in the background was her bodyguard, just in case he was needed. Although her nerves remained strained, she felt safer knowing that now she had two men to watch over her and to keep her safe.

Then Chalmers broke the news at dinner one night as they sat in a booth at the Night and Day Café on Highway 30 west of town.

"Guess what, guys?"

He pulled a newspaper clipping from his pocket, spread it out on the table in front of him, and slipped on his reading glasses.

"I guess I can dispense with future efforts from the private detective I hired!"

"What do you mean, Dad?"

"Listen to this. This is a clipping from the San Antonio Light newspaper that he sent me. I just got it today, along with his bill (naturally).

> A man wanted on charges of spousal abuse here in San Antonio was in custody Tuesday after leading deputies on a wild chase, authorities said yesterday. Jonathan Dietrich, 30, no address available, is being held at the county jail with bail set at $50,000. He is charged with aggravated felony assault on his wife, the former Nancy West, a registered nurse and a major in the Army Medical Service Corps. Until recently her duty station was at Brooke Army Hospital. Law officers had been looking for Dietrich for some days without success.
> Then an alert officer noticed a 1965 Plymouth that had failed to stop at a traffic light. Giving chase, he ordered the driver to pull over. Dietrich fled, at times his vehicle reached speeds up to 65 mph on crowded city streets. Other deputies also gave chase. In the 1500 block of Broadway, Dietrich lost control of his car which then struck a utility pole. He fled the scene on foot but was quickly captured. When officers searched his car they found quantities of marijuana.

Now in addition to the spousal abuse charge, he faces the added charges of aggravated fleeing and eluding, driving with a suspended license, and possession of controlled substances.

There!" Chalmers said with a smile, pulling off his glasses."That'll keep our boy busy and out of trouble for a good long while. I'm going to see what I can do about suggesting to the judge that he come down hard on the man. I have some legal contacts in San Antonio who ought to be able to help us in this. Congratulations, Nancy. Now you and Doug can think about leading a normal life."

* * * * *

Doug had been back from Washington, D.C. only a day or two when Cecil Currey walked up on the porch of the Andrews home, rang the bell, and asked to speak with Major Andrews.

Invited inside, Doug took him into the library where they sank deeply into two butter leather covered chairs. Charlotte brought them coffee. "There now. That's better," Doug said. "How may I help you, Dr. Currey?"

"Major, you are the most popular citizen that this town has ever had. Did you know that the mayor is planning to have a 'Doug Andrews Day' about two weeks from today? There will be bands, parades, fireworks, distinguished visitors, important speakers, and, of course, you–that is, if he ever gets up the courage to tell you what he wants to do." Currey chuckled.

Doug had been leaning forward, elbows on his knees. Now he sat back in alarm. "You've got to be kidding me, Dr. Currey! I'm no hero. Never was. Never will be. I don't want people in town to think of me that way."

"Nevertheless, that's what is going to happen. But that's not why I called. I was not exaggerating when I said that you are the most important person to ever have lived in Central City. No one else has ever been featured in newspaper write-ups across the country and even overseas, no one else has ever been on the cover of <u>Time</u> and <u>Newsweek</u>. There have been precious few who ever achieved the rank of major. Most in this community served as privates or airmen

146

or seamen and got out of the military as fast as they could. And certainly no one else has ever been awarded the Silver Star and, more importantly, the Medal of Honor. You may not be aware of it, but some ministers in town have even used you as an illustration in their sermons, likening you to Lazarus who came back from the dead."

Doug's face showed his horror. "Oh my God," he rumbled. "Oh my God. This has got to be stopped. It can't be allowed to go on."

"How exactly do you think you could stop it, Major Andrews? You <u>are</u> like Lazarus. You <u>did</u> come back from the dead. Hell, I attended your funeral in the Presbyterian Church down the block. I listened to the chaplain pronounce a blessing upon your soul. I saw your coffin carried out of the church. I rode in a procession out to the cemetery. I saw your coffin being committed to the earth. I heard a soldier sound Taps on his bugle and saw the honor guard fire salutes to you. I can even take you out there now and show you a headstone with your name engraved on it. No one in this town is going to leave you in peace. Everyone is excited about having a Doug Andrews Day."

"Stop," Andrews said. "That's enough. That's more than enough."

"Major, you must be one of the few in town who haven't heard about it. I know your father and mother approve. I know Laura gets starry-eyed whenever she thinks about you getting this honor in your own home town. Nancy thinks it's wonderful and that you really deserve to have a day set aside to honor you. No one of them has talked to you about it because the mayor told them he wanted the privilege of telling you." Currey smiled. "There is even a movement to put up a statue of you in South Park."

Doug slumped in his chair, sadly shaking his head back and forth. Through his mind flashed the image of a Vietnamese woman trying to run to him on legs that had no feet, reaching, grabbing, gibbering.

"Dr. Currey, I am not a goddam hero and don't want to be thought of as one."

147

"Well Major, I don't really think there is a hell of a lot you can do about it. And since that is so, I come to my reason for stopping by. I want to sit with you for several sessions, talking with you about your experiences and tape recording what you say. All that preliminary to writing a biographical book about . . . ."

"No!" said Doug holding his hand out, palm forward. "Absolutely not. Think about it. I 've been offered contracts with three different publishers willing to give me a six-figure advance if I'll sign with them to write my own account. They'll even supply a ghost writer. I refused. Told them I wasn't interested. My answer to you is the same I gave them. No. No. And No."

He stood and, reluctantly, Currey stood with him.

"Well, Major, you are going to make this harder for me but you won't stop me from chronicling your adventures. Much is in the public record. More is in the minds of those soldiers who have known you. Then there is Master Sergeant Szigmond out at Fort Lewis. He has already given me a conditional o.k. on interviewing him."

Currey's face brightened.

"You know, Major, I have already written two books. Made my boss, the president down at Nebraska Wesleyan very happy. As one of my colleagues would say, 'Nothing Mickey Mouse about that.' Now I am going to write a third. The first two were biographical studies of Benjamin Franklin. Guess what? I never once sat with the sage of Philadelphia for an interview! Not only did the scholarly world think highly of my effort but so did the reading public. Sold quite a number of them. . . ."

Doug's voice interrupted him. "I guess I may see you around town, sir. Let me walk you to the door."

* * * * *

It was Douglas MacArthur Andrews Day in Central City. The weather could not have been better: sunny with a few clouds and a light breeze with the temperature in the low 80s. The throng that had assembled was in a party mood, jubilant. Many found places to sit on the aluminum bleachers that had been erected for them. Hundreds of others stood along the sidewalks or huddled in twos and threes near the bleachers. Some strolled along in front of the Main Street stores, window shopping until it was time for the event to begin. Everyone smiled. There were handshakes and hugs and back slapping. Loud laughter often broke out. Everyone was ready to watch the spectacle on that October 15, 1970.

Reporters for the Nonpareil and Republican, the two local newspapers, were busily taking notes. Joining them were reporters from large city dailies: the Omaha World Herald, the Lincoln Journal and Star, the Washington Post, the Denver Post and a dozen others, including the Los Angeles Times. Camera crews checked their equipment while sound men positioned microphones. They had come to Central City at the behest of ABC, CBS, and NBC. Nationally known television 'talking heads' interviewed local citizens in a desultory way as possible filler material and as a means of passing time until things began to happen.

The center for this excitement was the town Triangle. Highway 30, or Main Street, had been cordoned off with traffic routed through residential districts so that the crowd could gather at the place that had so often been used for public meetings in past decades. It had been there, for example, that a 1944 crowd decided to donate the tall fountain that graced the Triangle to a scrap drive to be used for war purposes. That same day they gave the Spanish American War cannon located in North Park for the same reason.

Now they came to give honor to this favorite son. Chalmers Andrews was known and respected throughout the state. It was little wonder that many whom he had known as a state senator or as a result of his law practice, came to share in Chalmers' joy. Others who had met Charlotte through her participation in GROW, the anti-war group the full name of which was Get Rid of War, came to see her son praised. Laura's old sorority friends came in large numbers. It was the least they could do for a sister. Nancy and all the Andrews family sat on the platform in honored places, smiling and happy for the events of the day. That was not all. The governor and lieutenant governor were there. All were a little surprised that the Pentagon had not sent a representative. Those who came from out of town were

149

also surprised at the lack of accommodations: a small old hotel or the shabby run-down Crawford Motel. Little else was available so many drove to Grand Island, twenty-two miles to the west, to find a decent night's rest.

The festivities began. School had been dismissed for the day so that the children could march in a parade. It began at South Ward and moved north to Main Street, then west until the boys and girls reached the State Theater. Then they turned south and, when they reached the laundry, they were dismissed to find places in the crowd for themselves, to hunt for parents, or to skip away for their own fun. Marching in front of these children was the high school band, proudly stepping in unison as they moved down the highway, resplendent in their uniforms. Following along came aging men of Merrick County's chapter of the Foreign Legion. After the parade ended, members of the local Veterans of Foreign Wars chapter fired a blank shell in a small cannon they had borrowed for use that day. It was small town America at its best.

The mayor strode to the podium and adjusted the microphone.

"Ladies and gentlemen. We are gathered here this day to honor a native son of this town . . . ." After a few more words, he dropped a bombshell on Doug who was waiting out of sight nearby. "We have not only one, but two of our town boys here with us this day. The last time he came home he did so to preach a funeral in the Presbyterian Church. It was not a happy occasion. Today he is back, having taken leave from his duties as commandant of the Army's Chaplain School." He turned and beckoned. Chaplain (Colonel) Paul Eastley, wearing his military dress blues, walked up the steps to the podium, smiled, and asked a blessing on those there that day and upon the United States of America. Before taking his seat on the platform, he added that "The last time I came back to town it was to bury Caesar. This time I have come to praise him." The allusion to Shakespeare's play was a little too remote for most of those who heard him but still they clapped enthusiastically.

The mayor introduced the governor of the state, who made several remarks. After him came another soldier, Master Sergeant

Jan Lech Szigmond, also wearing dress blues, invited to be present that day as a special favor to his longtime friend. Doug was elated when he learned Szigmond was to be present. After the ceremony he planned to take him home, keep him there a few days, and entertain him as best he could before Szigmond had to leave again for the West Coast and his duties there. The next speaker was the president of the University of South Florida who had traveled to town from Tampa, Florida to congratulate this famous alumnus of the school. Several other speakers offered brief remarks. Then the mayor introduced the man they all had been waiting for: Major Douglas MacArthur Andrews.

"People, let's all give him a real Central City welcome!"

The crowd thundered its applause, clapping and hooting, whistling and shouting. They watched as the major, also in dress blues, walked out of the bank on the corner of the Triangle and marched stiffly across the street to the platform, mounted the steps, and stood before the microphones. The gold braid on his sleeves and the gold stripes on his trouser legs shimmered in the sunlight. His four rows of ribbons were mounted on his left breast just under his paratrooper wings and his Combat Infantry Badge. His shoes gleamed. The day before he had gotten a close haircut. He looked every inch a soldier, but the most impressive sight for those watching was the star spangled blue ribbon that hung around his neck, supporting the Medal of Honor.

Doug stood silently, gazing impassionately out on all those assembled in the Triangle. He felt more than a little embarrassed. They all thought he was a hero. He was not. They thought him brave. He was not. They thought him worthy of the decoration around his neck. He was not. He had accepted it only at the insistence of Szigmond. The ribbon felt like an anvil hanging around his neck. His only achievement had been to allow his soldiers to run amok in Yen Song (3) and then to be butchered by the Vietnamese Viet Cong. Oh yes. And with the help of Jan Szigmond he had escaped from prison, something he could never have done on his own. When he took his commission years ago and later when he went to Viet Nam he had sworn to be a good officer and to make a difference in the lives of those he led in battle. He had not done so. He was a failure.

Yet here in front of him were all these people expecting to hear a speech. He began in a halting way.

"My friends . . . and all of you who have gathered here this day, I thank you for what you have done for me. I want you to know I did not deserve this. But still I thank you. I came here today prepared to say a few words to you" and he held up a page of notes "but I don't know how I can say them to you. There is one thing I can do. I can introduce you to the man who should be wearing this Medal of Honor." He turned to Szigmond and called him forward. When the sergeant stood beside him, Doug put his arm around him and said, "This man is my friend. He taught me most of what I know about being a soldier. He saved my life many times. He taught me how to endure. He showed me the way to escape from North Viet Nam. He led me back to our own lines, south of the 17th Parallel. Ever since I met him he has encouraged me. He is the grandest soldier I have ever met."

Blinded by tears, Doug turned to Szigmond and hugged him and then moved back to his seat on the platform. The crowd thundered its approval.

Szigmond stood in place. When the crowd quieted, he spoke into the microphone. "My Lieutenant . . . I vill alvays think of him as my lieutenant . . . . is too bashful of a man. He deserves the decorations he wears. He is a hero. Thank you." And Szigmond turned away as the crowd once again went into a paroxysm of congratulatory noise.

Chaplain Eastley offered a benediction. A bugler from the high school band tooted his horn enthusiastically.

The mayor announced that the ceremony was over and those gathered in the Triangle began to dissipate. Doug was surrounded by family and other well wishers.

* * * * *

Short moments before, an Army drab sedan carrying three men came into Central City from the south on the old KND, the Kansas, Nebraska, Dakota Highway, now called Highway 14. It edged its way to the south side of the Triangle and parked. It was behind and below the speakers' platform and so no one on the stand or even in the crowd gave the car any particular notice.

Those inside sat quietly, pensively, until the ceremony ended. Then they got out of the car and walked toward the speakers' stand. They were three: a full colonel, a captain, and a command sergeant major. The two officers wore the branch insignia of the Judge Advocate General's Corps–JAG. The sergeant wore the insignia of the Military Police.

Pushing their way through the crowd they finally managed to stand beside Major Andrews. Doug was startled to see these strange men in uniform. He wondered who had invited them? What was their purpose? Humorless, the colonel spoke to him.

"Please come with us. We should move to a more private place. I don't believe you will want others to hear this."

Excusing himself, Doug followed the three men across the Triangle to stand beside their car.

The colonel turned and granite-faced looked at him. "This must be done properly and in order. Are you Major Douglas MacArthur Andrews?"

"Yessir. Of course. You must know that. What's this all about?"

"Major Andrews. An indictment has been filed in which you have been charged with encouraging your troops and yourself participating in the wanton murder of over two hundred noncombatant civilian inhabitants of the Vietnamese hamlet of Yen Song (3) in the Republic of South Viet Nam. We hereby arrest you and will transport you to the Disciplinary Barracks at Fort Leavenworth in Kansas to be held there pending and during your court martial. If you cannot afford one, a military defense lawyer will be provided you. Perhaps you would now like to say goodbye to your family before we begin the journey south. And take off all those medals. You disgrace them."

Underneath his feet, Doug could feel the earth move.

* * * * *

CHAPTER NINE

"I mourn in my complaint and make a noise . . . for they cast iniquity upon me and in wrath they hate me."–Psalms LV, 2b, 3b. "...the tumult of those that rise up against thee increaseth continually."–Psalms LXXIV, 23b. "Though he fall he shall not be utterly cast down, for the Lord upholdeth him with his hand."--Psalms XXXVII, 24.

Major Douglas MacArthur Andrews, still wearing his beribboned dress blue uniform, stood rigidly at attention, heels locked, before the desk of Fort Leavenworth's provost marshal, a full colonel. Somewhere, a world away now, it was still "his" day and most of those who congregated in Central City's Triangle for the celebration remained ignorant of the fact that their hero was now under military arrest. The colonel's face was unreadable, perhaps because in the course of his career he had seen and heard everything and now believed nothing.

"You, Sir, are now assigned to the Disciplinary Barracks here. But you are not sentenced here, at least not yet. Military arrest is different in this way from that practiced in the civilian world. You will not be confined except in a limited way and you will not be under physical restraint.. You will accept quarters in the Visiting Officers' Quarters. You will have a two room suite, with refrigerator, wet bar, and television. You may go freely in and out of the VOQ, but you may not stray off its grounds. The edge of its campus is the limit of your ability to move freely. There is one exception to this rule. On Sundays you may attend worship services at the post chapel if you so desire, but then must immediately return to the VOQ accompanied by your MP escort. Do you understand these provisions?"

"Yes, Sir."

"You will now be sent to Quartermaster where you will draw– and pay for–your regulation set of uniforms, to include BDUs. An MP will accompany you. At all times, whenever it is necessary for you to leave the confines of the VOQ an MP will accompany you.

155

The uniform of the day here is the Battle Dress Uniform. You will wear it at all times until the start of your court martial, at which time you will wear dress greens. Do you understand?"

"Yes, Sir."

"In a day or so you will be taken to the hospital where you will undergo a psychiatric evaluation to determine whether or not you are fit to stand trial. Anything and everything you tell the psychiatrist will be confidential. Only his final recommendation will be seen by others. Do you understand?"

"Yes, Sir."

"I understand that you come from a very well-off family, yet regulations require me to tell you this. If you cannot afford a lawyer, one of the Judge Advocate General's people will be assigned to defend you. Such a lawyer will defend you to the best of his ability, but having no stake in the outcome will probably mean that you might want to consider using a civilian lawyer. I am not allowed to recommend any specific individuals. Do you understand?"

"Sir, yes, Sir. My father is a lawyer. He is currently seeking military certification so that he may act as my counsel . . . ."

"Do you realize that his emotional investment in his son may well skew his ability to defend you?"

"Yes, Sir. But he is asking to have co-counsel also."

"Very well. That is your right and your choice. Be aware that all proceedings against you will be conducted with strict adherence to *The Uniform Code of Military Justice* and *The Manual for Courts-Martial*. They contain all the details, all the procedures, all the guidance that those who sit in judgment over you will need. There is a problem facing the prosecution however. The UCMJ is silent as to "war crimes." It does not mention them. It does, however, have much to say about murder, for which there is no statute of limitations. It states that murder is a felony of the first degree, although mitigating circumstances can lower the degree of that crime. Now, if you understand all these things I have told you, then sign and date this paper. It is a simple form stating that you have been briefed on what will be facing you here."

"Yes, Sir. One question, Sir. How soon will the court be convened?"

"This will be a general court-martial. As such it takes a little longer to set it in motion. I also understand that in your case, prosecution witnesses from Viet Nam are being sought and, if located, will be transported here at government expense to testify against you. The Vietnamese government has been asked to help and it is trying to locate survivors. Supposedly three inhabitants of the hamlet survived . . . ."

"Sir, I believe I am entitled to a speedy trial . . . ."

"Yes you are. And if that is your wish I will so note it and refer your request to proper authority. That's all . . . and Major? I hope things go well. I also served in Viet Nam. Two tours. I know how bad it can be when a unit has been under constant combat stress."

"Thank you, Sir. I appreciate that." Doug saluted, did an about face, and strode from the office. Outside the door a waiting MP fell in step with him.

* * * * *

Four months had passed, time Chalmers spent frantically trying to develop a coherent and believable defense for his son. He was ready. So also was the prosecution. It was mid-January 1971 and the area around Leavenworth, Kansas was clothed in winter's silvered garments.

The trial was scheduled for the next day and Chalmers visited the courtroom to acquaint himself with its layout. He held in his hand a copy of the official order establishing the court-martial: "A general court-martial will convene at Headquarters, Fort Leavenworth, Kansas on 18 January 1971to try Major Douglas MacArthur Andrews, 02 326 469, presently assigned to the Disciplinary Barracks, Fort Leavenworth, on the charge of murder in the first degree, said murder having taken place in the village of My Yen, at the hamlet of Yen Song (3) in the Republic of Viet Nam on 12 February 1967. Then company commander of Alpha Company, 2nd Battalion, 11th Brigade, 23rd Infantry Division, Major Andrews did violate Article 118, Clause Three, of the Uniform Code of Military Justice, murder in the first degree. He did there engage in illegal acts demonstrative of a disregard for human life, causing the murder of an unknown number but at least ninety Oriental human beings, males and females, of various ages, whose names remain unknown, by shooting them or causing them to be shot by pistol, rifle, or machine gun fire or to be killed with hand grenades, incendiary devices, and bayonets."

Every time he read those words, Chalmers' heart thudded wildly. In less than a month, it would be four years since the alleged crime. He looked around. The room to be used for this court-martial was stark. No pictures or paintings graced the walls, painted in a dirty beige. The furniture was minimal. A table covered with a white cloth would serve the presiding judge, a full colonel. Against the wall, behind that table, sat a stand from which neatly hung an American flag. Near the table of the presiding judge was another, smaller one at which would sit the recording clerk. To the judge's right was a table that would be used by the prosecution and opposite was the table for the defense. To the judge's left and quite near him were two additional tables at which the members of the trial board would sit. There were seven empty chairs lined up there. Chalmers stood before that table for a few moments recalling that because of the decorations worn by his son, the members of that board would hold higher rank than was usually necessary.

The president of the board was to be a full colonel from JAG corps. That meant that presumably he was himself a lawyer. Five other members would be lieutenant colonels, drawn from a variety of Army branches. Chalmers hoped that infantry would be well represented among them. If not infantry, then artillery or armor or even engineers– the combat branches of the U.S. Army. Such men might well have more sympathy for a man charged with murder, who at the time of the alleged felony had been a young captain of infantry. Unlike civilian capital trials, unanimity among the jurors was not needed. Two-thirds could convict. During sessions of the trial an armed sergeant-at-arms in dress greens would guard the door to the room.

The bulk of the room was taken up by seating for those who would attend. A good many folding chairs had been set up to accommodate them. Chalmers stood among them and shivered as he thought of the upcoming trial. His son was fighting for his very life, for if convicted, he could be hung or executed by firing squad. He himself was fighting for the life of his heir, his beloved first-born. He could not afford to lose, yet he knew that the prosecuting team was capable and experienced. Even worse, the terrible story of the My Lai massacre was still fresh in everyone's mind. The deputy chief of staff of the army, Lieutenant General William Raymond Peers had been appointed by General William Westmoreland to investigate what had happened in that remote village and he had only recently released his findings to the public, a thick book entitled *The Peers Commission Report on the My Lai Massacre*. Chalmers had worked his way through its pages, hoping to find material that might help in Doug's defense. Instead he had encountered General Peers' contention that My Lai was not an aberration but had been a rather commonplace occurrence due to illegal actions by U.S. soldiers in Viet Nam. He bowed his head in momentary prayer.

* * * * *

Eventide that day came like Carl Sandburg's fog—on little cat feet. The snow everywhere muffled sounds, except for the passing of an occasional car equipped with tire chains. Inside his room in the VOQ Doug Andrews prepared for bed although he realized he probably would be unable to sleep. Tomorrow would be too big a day to allow for that.

As he undressed he recalled his two counseling sessions with the head of the post's medical psychiatry section. Doug confessed to the psychiatrist appointed to examine him that he was beset by dreams and images of Yen Song (3). They were, he said, so real that it seemed as if he was actually back at the hamlet. The physician replied that a great many men who had seen combat in Viet Nam had the same problem. The medical fraternity, he said, had come up with a name for such suffering. It was now known as PTSD–post traumatic stress disorder–and it sometimes traumatized men so thoroughly that a number had committed suicide or murder. Others had turned to alcohol or drugs. Some alienated their children, their wives, their parents. A

159

few had dropped completely out of society, turning their backs on all that had once seemed precious to them and now lived on the edge, cadging food, smokes and beer money from sympathetic passersby, sleeping under bridges and interstate viaducts. The information was interesting but Doug didn't quite see how knowing that others had his problem was going to lay his own devils to rest.

Andrews lay down on his bed, wondering if those inside the nearby prison were as comfortable. Soon, perhaps, he would have opportunity to find out. At some point that very night he drifted into a tormented sleep and he found himself back at Yen Song (3). Through his troubled sleep flitted dark chaotic images of that day when he not only lost control of himself but of his men. It was evening and the sun was setting, pillowed on far off treetops. In the shadows were hideous, menacing forces that reached out for his soul. On the ground lay gory, mangled things that squealed and flopped and wriggled, all taking much too long to die. For some, fresh gore flooded from gaping wounds. The fruit of their agony poured onto the ground, turning it viscid. Doug noted that the setting sun was now swallowed by voracious mists, and above him hovered a fog-dimmed moon. Nearby lay a mere used by the hamlet's people to flood their paddies, the air above its stagnant waters alive with fluttering insects. On all sides Doug heard the sound of battle, the crump of grenades, the chatter of machine guns, the constant pounding of rifles, all interspersed with the cries of wounded and dying animals and the shrieks for mercy made by the women, the children, the old men of Yen Song (3). Overhead he heard the flutter of a helicopter that hovered momentarily and then quickly turned and disappeared in the distance.

A comment by Nietzsche came to him, one he had read a hundred years before in a philosophy class at the University of South Florida. He knew the words were not quite remembered correctly, but he thought he recalled the gist of the dark philosopher's phrases:

> Whoever fights monsters should see to it that in the process he does not become a monster. And when he looks into the abyss, the abyss looks back at him.

That empty, cursed, bottomless pit loomed before him. He saw an old man of the hamlet scrambling up the loom of a nearby hill, and he fired his weapon at him. His target, like Jill of the old nursery rhyme, came tumbling down and then lay still, limbs akimbo. Doug screamed in fear, remorse, anger and pain.

* * * * *

It was a Sunday and Doug sat in the day room of the VOQ surrounded by his family–father, mother, sister, and his loved one, Nancy. They had all just returned from worship services at the post chapel and his mother had queried him about the armed MP who seemed always to accompany him. The women had driven down to Fort Leavenworth the day before to spend time with him. Nancy had earlier asked to stay all the time until the court-martial was over, but Chalmers had intervened.

"Nancy, I know your heart is with Doug in this matter, but he and I need to spend most of our time in preparation for the trial. We rehearse. We brainstorm. We research. We seek counsel from learned men. There isn't much time left after a day spent doing those things. I think it would be better for you to stay in Central City and come down on some sort of regular basis with Charlotte and Laura. Maybe you can work with Charlotte in her GROW organization to help pass the time. Is that o.k.?"

"Yes, Dad," she said.

Chalmers preened at the name she called him. For nearly four years he had been hoping that one day she would become his daughter-in-law. He hoped she would one day feel comfortable enough with him to refer to him as "Dad." Then it all seemed to end when she married Jonathan Dietrich. She and the Andrews family had slowly drifted apart due to the distance between their homes and under pressure from Jonathan. Chalmers' hopes were resurrected when he retrieved her from the women's shelter in San Antonio after she had fled from Jonathan's "hearth and home," as the old phrase had it. If she had not done so she might well now be dead. Then she had called him and he had taken her into the bosom of his family. Now, in this time of grave difficulties she had called him "Dad." It warmed his soul. He smiled

161

at Nancy and squeezed her hand. "Thanks, sweetheart. Maybe you won't be upset with me when I tell you that I have already filed papers on your behalf seeking a divorce from Jonathan."

"I love you, Dad. Thank you so very much."

He looked at Charlotte and Laura. "That also goes for you ladies," he said with a smile. "Don't even think of trying to come down here to stay until the trial is over. Nancy would distract Doug. You two would do the same with me. Our boy here needs all the help I can give him." He leaned over and kissed his wife. You and Laura mean everything to me, but Doug and I have this huge obstacle to overcome, and we have formidable opposition from those who for their own purposes want to railroad Doug into lifelong confinement or worse. O.K.?" The three women managed to shake their heads in affirmation.

* * * * *

During those weeks Doug and Chalmers were regularly besieged by print and television reporters wanting interviews so they could reveal "his" side of the story to an interested public. Most such requests were refused but once a week, Doug and Chalmers would select one individual and spend perhaps fifteen minutes telling of recent events. At times when there had been nothing new, they told how strange it was that a Medal of Honor recipient should have to bear such ignominy, adding to the psychological burdens Doug carried as a result of his imprisonment and long months of torture. Many times, Doug wanted desperately to confess to such reporters that all the charges against him were just, that he was indeed a monster, but Chalmers kept a restraining hand on his son, preventing him from doing so.

"Let's wait, son. Let's let this slide until after the court-martial. Then, if you want, you can spend the rest of your life in some far off mission field atoning for your sins, real or imagined and praying to God for forgiveness. But putting you in prison or hanging you won't help, not either one of them."

Chalmers spent a good deal of time on the telephone conferring with other lawyers more experienced in defending clients facing trial on murder charges. One of those he consulted was a tall, rangy man who favored western wear and who lived in Montana. An experienced litigator, he had seldom ever lost a case even despite his having taken on some cases where all the facts seemed to point to the guilt of his client. Chalmers thought the advice he gave was good.

"Well, Chalmers, there are certain things you must do."

"Yes, Gary. I have a pencil waiting to write them down."

"First. Do absolutely nothing to alienate either the judge or the military board. Second. As a certified lawyer, be sure and get in the record that you are yourself a patriotic American who fought during World War II against the fascists and suffered wounds as a result. Third. Attack the prosecution with all the power that is within you. It is, you will say, a sort of crime in itself to punish this man who has suffered for his country, who has always tried to do his duty, who has been awarded a Medal of Honor. Fourth. Deny the validity of the charges. Stress that there may have been no crime actually committed. Then, if that falls flat, deny that the court has jurisdiction. The court will not concede those facts and you will lose that appeal. But it is important to have gotten it in the record. Fifth. Attack the prosecution's logic. Sixth. Explain all the alleged facts presented by your opponent in the most mitigating way possible. Seventh. Appeal to the consciences of those board members who are combat arms. Remind them, as if they needed any reminding, that 'war is hell.' Eighth. Be prepared to shout louder than the JAG lawyers. (A little joke there, my friend. You needn't jot that one down.) Then sit down and wait for the verdict. Chalmers? That may not be the best advice. But it is how I would handle it if I were your son's lawyer."

"Thanks, Gary. I appreciate it. And I owe you one."

* * * * *

One visitor came regularly, every Saturday, for some weeks. He seemed oblivious to Doug's coldness and each time he faced the major he again asked the same question.

"Doug? Are you going to cooperate with me in writing your story? As you know, much has happened since the first time I had this conversation with you. It is only fair for you to have your side of all

163

this told and I am just the one to do that for you. I know that sounds egotistical but I really am a good writer."

"No, Dr. Currey, I won't agree."

Not one to give up easily, Currey handed the major a copy of one of his books on Benjamin Franklin. "Here, Major. Read this when you have the time. It will give you an idea of my writing style. The Los Angeles <u>Times</u> review said that this history book 'reads like a novel.' You may change your mind."

Then on one of Currey's visits he found Chalmers and Doug together and so put his request to them both. Chalmers listened with interest as Doug shook his head negatively.

"Don't be so quick to say no, Doug," Chalmers volunteered. This may be something we need to think about. We need some venue to get your story out other than in newspapers and on short television reports where some talking head anchor gives you fifteen seconds and then says, 'in other news a tornado hit the community of Larned. There were no casualties . . . .' We need something more than that. Dr. Currey wouldn't be able to finish a book in the time left before the trial, but even the announcement that he is undertaking a story that will set the record straight once and for all may give the prosecution some little hesitation. Doug, we need all the help we can get!"

So it came to pass that the major agreed to talk to Dr. Currey, openly, completely, holding nothing back, reserving only the right to approve any text before it was released to a publisher and to insist on needed corrections. Currey was elated. His persistence had paid off. Doug was frightened, wondering how he was going to be able to speak of some of those events that haunted the very fiber of his soul.

* * * * *

People crowded into the court room when the doors opened. Among them were the loved ones of Major Douglas MacArthur Andrews: his mother Charlotte, his sister Laura, his beloved Nancy. They sat with frightened hearts and tear-stained faces. Nearby sat another Central Citian, Cecil Currey, waiting for the proceedings to begin and fiddling with his tape recorder, adjusting his directional microphone, putting his pencil and note pad in correct alignment. He planned to capture every word of the forthcoming trial in preparation for writing his book. He had contacted his agent after his conversation with Doug and Chalmers and his agent expressed keen interest in peddling a manuscript that would tell the complete tale of a story that had captivated the nation ever since Doug and Jan had managed to escape and reach American lines.

It took only a few days before the agent informed him that one of America's premier publishing companies wanted a contract. The company was willing to pay an advance of six figures. Currey quickly signed on the dotted line.

* * * * *

Doug stood at attention beside his father as those in the courtroom rose as the judge, followed by the seven members of the military Board filed into the room and took their assigned places. When those officers were seated, the judge spoke: "You may all be seated."

He then spoke to those in the room.

"This is a court-martial of Major Douglas MacArthur Andrews for the alleged crime of committing murder during the course of his duties as a company commander in Viet Nam. There is but one witness for the prosecution. It had wanted to use others. The government planned to call three survivors but the government of the Republic of Viet Nam has been unable to locate them. Thus the prosecution faces the difficult task of convicting Major Andrews on the basis of the testimony of corpses and on notes made shortly after the alleged incident by now Lieutenant Colonel, but then Major, Donald Stoddard, then Brigade Staff, 11th Brigade (Separate), 23rd Infantry Division, on the basis of a conversation he held with Lieutenant Colonel Jeremiah Barrett, Second Battalion commander, who unfortunately died shortly thereafter."

Doug looked at his father and winced. Chalmers patted him on the shoulder and whispered "It's o.k. It's o.k."

The judge looked at Chalmers. "Sir, it is your duty in this court-martial to represent the accused to the best of your ability consistent with the requirements of military justice. It is your responsibility to

165

see that the rights and obligations of the accused are maintained at all times."

He turned to the prosecution team headed by the JAG full colonel. "You, Sir, must prove to the members of this court-martial board, and to do so beyond a reasonable doubt, that the charges and specifications in this case are true. It is not necessary to convict this man for you to accomplish your military responsibility here. You must only see that justice is safeguarded, that a fair and impartial trial is held in accordance with the customs and traditions of the Army."

Now it was time for him to speak to the seven members of the military board.

"You must hear the evidence presented while simultaneously and consciously stifling anything you may have heard or read about this man and this case. Your only task is to insure that, if you come to believe that Major Andrews is guilty, he is given an appropriate punishment. I can't stress this fact enough. You must believe that he had full and complete knowledge of the rules of warfare and that he wilfully violated the Uniform Code of Military Justice. Now, if you gentlemen will stand, I will administer to you the oath to do your best, so help you God."

After that had been done, he turned to Major Andrews. "Will the accused please stand?"

Doug snapped to his feet.

"How do you plead to the charge and specification of this case in which you have allegedly violated the rules of land warfare and have committed murder?"

"Sir, I plead not guilty."

"Then let us begin."

* * * * *

The prosecuting colonel rose from his desk and stood before the seven members of the board.

"Gentlemen, it has long been the custom and practice of the United States Army that a person, entrusted with the great responsibility of commanding a unit, is therefore and thereafter <u>always</u> responsible for that unit's behavior until he is relieved from command by proper authority. A commander may take credit for successes but he must also bear the blame for failures. It is for this reason that some officers are promoted and others asked to resign.

"That tradition was not set aside when we entered into the conflict in Viet Nam. It is our purpose here to demonstrate that during his tour of duty in Viet Nam in 1966 and 1967, Major Andrews deliberately violated the Army's Law of Land Warfare and failed in his duties as a commander causing grievous harm and injury to the inhabitants of Yen Song (3), a hamlet of My Yen village.

"Article 501 of that Law of Land Warfare clearly states that commanders will be responsible for crimes, for atrocities committed by their troops against a nonresisting civilian population. All of Major Andrews' troops in the Second Platoon of Alpha Company were killed by enemy action. Had any survived, they too would be facing military trial. That is not to be. The only man we can punish is the one who bore responsibility for them all, Major Douglas MacArthur Andrews.

"Major Andrews had served in Viet Nam for nearly a year. His DEROS date was but a few days away. He had been in combat many times during that year. He knew the rules. If he needed a reminder he need only take from his pocket a plastic card authorized by General William Westmoreland on which was written in clear English that killing unarmed or unresisting or sick or wounded individuals— particularly if they were innocent civilians--was unacceptable behavior, punishable by courts-martial. At Yen Song (3), Major Andrews violated that Law and the Uniform Code of Military Justice. He knew what he was supposed to do and how he was supposed to act, and he wilfully turned his back on his responsibilities.

"Perhaps most damning of all is the evidence that he may himself have participated in the slaughter of the denizens of Yen Song (3). Only the death penalty can erase this blot upon the escutcheon of the military. We must show our ally, the Republic of Viet Nam and the countries of the world that American soldiers will not be allowed to act in this way."

* * * * *

Doug listened to all this spellbound. In his heart he believed the colonel spoke the truth. Not a day had gone by in the last four years when he was not plagued by the skeletal fingers of his memory. He nervously doodled on a pencil pad in front of him, occasionally glancing at his father who sat calmly at the table.

The JAG colonel called his only witness–Lieutenant Colonel Donald Stoddard. He held up a sheaf of papers.

"Colonel Stoddard? Are these true copies of the notes you made back in 1967 after the massacre?"

Stoddard took the pages from his hand, glanced through them, and then responded.

"Yes, Sir, they are."

The prosecutor then asked the judge for permission to have the notes Stoddard had made of the incident read into the trial record. The request was approved.

"Let's talk about the incident at Yen Song (3). Do you have certain knowledge that then Captain Douglas Andrews was present there?"

"Yes, Sir, I do."

"Colonel Stoddard, do you know Major Andrews well?"

"Yes, Sir, I believe so."

"Were you in Viet Nam at the same time as he?"

"Yes, Sir."

"Did you have frequent contact with him?"

"No, Sir. Our jobs allowed only for infrequent contacts."

"How did you come by your knowledge of the massacre at Yen Song (3)?"

"The facts were told to me by Doug's battalion commander, Lieutenant Colonel Jeremiah Barrett."

"What did he tell you?"

"He said that he and the brigade commander, Colonel Vernon Moore, flew over Yen Song (3) during the massacre in the command and control helicopter used by Moore and saw U.S. troops firing at the people of the hamlet. If I remember correctly, he said 'There was blood everywhere.'"

"U.S. troops firing?"

"Yessir."

"As I recall, the information was given out at the time that the dead villagers were killed by the Viet Cong so that the communists could claim that U.S. troops had acted in a callous barbaric way."

"Yessir, that's what happened."

"So this was not true?"

"Nossir."

"Why didn't General, then Colonel, Moore land the helicopter and attempt to gain control of the situation?" "Sir, Colonel Barrett said he refused to do so."

"Do you know why?"

"Sir, I know what Colonel Barrett told me. He said that Colonel Moore didn't want to have any real or actual knowledge of what was going on at ground level. That way if there was any later inquiry, he could truthfully say that he was unaware of the situation."

Print reporters in the room scribbled furiously as TV cameramen concentrated on the images caught by their lenses. Others quickly fled the room, frantic to find a telephone to call in this new information. As they spoke to colleagues back at their stations and newspapers, they could envision the coming headlines:

GENERAL VERNON MOORE ACCUSED OF COVER UP IN YEN SONG (3)

Lieutenant Colonel Donald Stoddard, was called today as a witness for the prosecution in the court-martial of Major Douglas MacArthur Andrews, a Viet Nam veteran recently awarded the Medal of Honor by President Johnson. The trial is now under way at Fort Leavenworth, Kansas and Major Andrews has been charged with allegedly murdering innocent civilians in a small Vietnamese hamlet four years ago. Colonel Stoddard dropped a bombshell in court today when he testified that General Vernon "Savage" Moore deliberately withheld and covered up information that he was aware of what had happened at Yen Song (3).

The Pentagon has strongly denied the charges, but agreed that it will convene an investigating committee to look into the matter. General Moore has not been available for comment, all attempts to reach him having failed. His aide has assured this reporter that there is absolutely no truth to the allegation.

Aware that he had opened "a can of worms" with his questioning, the JAG colonel quickly moved on to other questions. He kept Stoddard on the stand for nearly an hour before excusing him. He next handed the judge and each of the seven board members a packet containing graphic photographs of the massacre site and the mass graves where the dead had been buried by their neighbors. Then he turned to the judge.

"Sir, the prosecution rests."

Now it was Chalmers' turn, as counsel for the accused, to modify, excuse, or explain away whatever impressions the prosecutor had instilled in the minds of the board members.

"Judge, gentlemen of the Board, I stand before you today as an old soldier of long ago for I enlisted in the Army infantry in early 1942 and remained there until February 1945. I was wounded during the battles for the Huertgen Forest and convalesced at an Army hospital in England.

"But that was all long ago and things I once knew well have become dim with the passage of decades. I therefore ask your tolerance if I seem ignorant of Army rules and traditions. Any mistakes are unintentional.

"Sirs, it is obvious that the prosecution has done an excellent job of describing the duties and responsibilities of leadership. I commend them. But that was never the question. The right question to ask is whether Major Douglas MacArthur Andrews is guilty of murder or whether, in the name of his country, he killed our enemies while in Viet Nam. Enemies that he faced time and again. Enemies who tried every way possible to kill him and his men. We know that he and thousands of other lieutenants and captains just like him have been sent there under direct orders and told to defend the interests of the Republic of Viet Nam at all costs. That is also why we have sent thousands upon thousands of our young draftees to fight there as enlisted men.

"The alleged problems at Yen Song (3) occurred in a foreign country during a military operation in time of war. I am thus not even certain that this court has any jurisdiction in this matter. Nor am I convinced that a crime actually took place. Death occurred, yes. But a crime? The prosecution has not proven that my client is guilty of any crime at all. At that time Major Andrews and all his men faced the worst kind of danger, imminent death at any moment, death from unknown assailants, dangers they could not see. They knew the fear caused by sudden silences in a jungle alive with noise; they knew about footfalls drawing close to the protective wire of their perimeter when on moonless nights they could not see where the enemy was or how many of them there were. They knew the bladder-emptying terror caused by enemy weapons suddenly blasting at them when they mistakenly wandered into a booby-trapped kill zone. Three of their comrades died within minutes right in their midst on that fateful day at Yen Song (3), Second Lieutenant Norman Crosse and Staff Sergeant Leroy Johnson and Specialist George Catlett, all killed when no one expected any combat action.

Chalmers now launched into unknown waters. Even he did not know many of the details of what he was about to say to the court. What he did know was third hand. Those facts had been told by members of Second Platoon to Captain Andrews after the death of Lieutenant Norman Crosse when Andrews had suddenly joined them on a dead run from his position with First Platoon. In turn, Doug had searched his memory for their words and told his father everything he could remember about their testimony. Now Chalmers began to tell the story of that day.

"If any man can be said to have a 'clean death,' then that is what happened to Johnson and Catlett, each killed quickly by a single shot. That is not what happened to Second Lieutenant Norman Crosse. He was torn utterly to pieces by an exploding bomb salvaged from a battlefield by Viet Cong warriors and buried along the path leading to Yen Song (3). His injuries were so sickening that it roils my mind

171

even to think of them. Metal shards and blast severed Crosse's legs above the knees, shredding the amputated limbs into bits of frothy pink tissue. The explosive force continued upward, ripping clothing, skin and muscle wall from his abdomen, sucking ten feet of intestine after it. Blast wrenched the greasy, gray gut that remained out of its cavity and spilled it onto the bloodied ground . . . ."

The JAG colonel rose to his feet. "Judge, I protest. While all this is interesting–and sad–it does not bear on the situation facing us: was Captain Andrews guilty of murder or not? That is the only question and testimony should be restricted to material dealing with it.

The judge looked at Chalmers.

"Sir, it is important to discover what went on in the minds of those Americans at Yen Song (3) that day so we will know their motives."

"I accept your reasoning, Sir, and the objection is denied. Make sure, however, that your comments are apt ones."

"Yes, Sir. Thank you. As I was saying . . . the explosion still expanded upward, metal slicing off Crosse's left hand in a jagged cut and tearing out sections of skin and muscle on his right arm from wrist to elbow, exposing glistening white bone quickly reddened by a rush of blood.

"The force also tore off his right ear and a tiny sliver of steel opened his cheek and forehead. More blood spilled out. The explosion snatched his helmet off, forcing his head back so sharply that, according to the military autopsy, it fractured three vertebrae in his neck. All this happened in two-fifths of a second–the longest time in the short life of Second Lieutenant Norman Crosse.

"His last words? They went something like this: 'Kill me. For God's sake, kill me. Please help me. Oh my God, please.' This was a large man, this was a very strong man, this was a man with a superb, magnificent voice who hoped one day to sing opera professionally. This is a man who only recently had arrived in-country. Now he was a dying ruin amidst the paddies of Viet Nam.

"And this was the beginning. This happened on a day when no one in Captain Andrews' company expected to meet up with a civilian population. ARVN was supposed to have evacuated all its people from this zone so that Second Battalion could undertake a thoroughgoing examination of the area in hopes of discovering the whereabouts of the Viet Cong 48th Local Force Battalion, a unit that had given much trouble to the 11th Brigade, a unit that had been sought time and again without success.

"Captain Andrews was not even with Second Platoon when this occurred. He was moving with First Platoon, some distance to the north when he heard the explosion. Beside him was his executive officer, First Lieutenant Jim Davis, and Captain Andrews, like any good commander, gave orders as to the way he wanted his platoons deployed. Then, at a dead run, he moved toward the noise. It was what happened next that is the subject of this court.

"Sir? I would like to recall Lieutenant Colonel Donald Stoddard to the stand."

The board members at their tables looked at one another with some surprise. For the defense to call a prosecution witness to the stand was always risky business.

"I remind you, Colonel, that you are still under oath."

"Yes, Sir."

"Can you give us any indication of what happened next?"

"Not really, Sir. I wasn't there."

"What then was the basis for your notes that have played such a large part in these proceedings?"

"They were based upon comments made to me by the battalion commander, Lieutenant Colonel Jeremiah Barrett."

"I understand that Colonel Barrett had been drinking when he spoke with you."

"Yessir, he had."

"Was he inebriated?"

"Sir, he had at least five double shots of whiskey while we sat in the officer's club and I listened to him. He had also been drinking before we accidentally met that night. During our conversation I believe his alcohol level was sufficiently high that he was no longer aware of who he was talking to. I was just a neutral body on which he poured out his troubles."

"I see. So those notes were made based on the testimony of a drunken sot whose mind may well have been troubled by demons we can only imagine and which might well have had nothing to do directly with Yen Song (3). Thank you, Colonel. Now. What can you tell us about general conditions on the 'Pinko Peninsula' where all this happened? As a member of Brigade staff you should have been well acquainted with the situation."

"Yessir. The Brigade had been trying to take out the 48th Local Force Battalion for some time. We were never able to make contact. They would hit one of our separate units and then run. The VC had caused a number of casualties, wounded and killed. So Colonel Moore, our Brigade commander, planned another effort to roust them. He called it 'Operation Barrett' since it would be the Second Battalion that would lead the hunt. Then Barrett named the landing zone that would be used LZ Mildred in honor of his wife. Sir, before the planning had ended, Captain Andrews asked for an artillery preparation on the site and demanded that ARVN evacuate all villagers. Orders were sent to ARVN but the artillery request was denied. Colonel Moore said it was too late to work the request into the plan. Captain Andrews was agitated about that decision."

"Thank you. So you are saying that the assault may have lacked essential elements for safe entry and exit?"

"Yes, Sir.

"Do you happen to know anything about Captain Andrews' frame of mind at that time?"

"Yessir. He had been in constant contact with the enemy for nearly a year. When his required six months in combat drew to a close, he insisted on extending for another six months. He once told me that he had learned a lot and that there was no point in giving his job to some 'newby' who might well get himself and his men killed while taking his 'on the job training.'"

174

Stoddard continued. "He lost something like twenty-five pounds in that year. At one point he was sent to a hospital to recuperate from several ailments which plagued him. He resisted the orders sending him there, believing his men might not be safe without him. He was a very conscientious platoon leader and later a company commander. On more than one occasion he insisted to me that his primary responsibility was to insure that his troops avoided death or injury and that they got home in one piece. It grated on him when enemy action caused several of them to die or suffer wounds from combat actions. Those losses built up in him a real sense of guilt. He was grief-stricken more and more as the weeks went by."

Stoddard's brow wrinkled in concentration as he tried to determine what to say next.

"I have known Major Andrews since we were both in the same officer basic class. He has always acted with the utmost integrity. He has not cut corners. He has not made excuses. He has always been professional. But before the assault on My Yen he was simply worn out. Too much pain. Too much sorrow. Too much guilt. Too tired. Too sick. You name it, Sir. It was all too much. I saw that. In a meeting just prior to the assault I noted great disillusionment with the war, with Viet Nam, with the Army, with himself. I went to his battalion commander and told him that I thought Andrews needed to be dropped from the assault plan. He refused. I then went to the Brigade commander and asked that he be reassigned to a noncombat slot. He had spent long enough in hell."

He continued. "The brigade commander called me an interfering little pipsqueak and said there was no way he was going to replace a proven 'Cong killer.' I felt as if I had failed my friend."

"Was this the brigade commander you earlier referred to when the prosecution was asking you questions? The man who covered up his knowledge of what happened at Yen Song (3)?"

"Yessir."

"What else can you tell the court about Major Andrews?"

'Just one thing more, Sir. On several occasions we had arguments about what was and was not permissible for our military to

175

do in Viet Nam. The first time this came up was when we were both assigned to the 90th Overseas Replacement and Processing Center at Fort Lewis, Washington. I had just told the trainees who were POR, processing for overseas replacement, that Army practice allowed our troops, if they were fired upon, to use full firepower against any village or hamlet from which the shots had come. Full firepower. Automatic weapons. Grenades. Mortars. Artillery. Napalm. Bombs. Full firepower. I said they were authorized to protect themselves in any way necessary. They could enter that enemy ville firing their weapons, killing anything and everything that moved. They could torch the hootches, burn the crops, poison the well. All in reaction to even one single shot fired at them. So far as I know, Sir, that is still standard practice. Major Andrews vehemently disagreed. We almost came to blows. Right there in front of the trainees. He also lectured me more than once about what he called St. Augustine's doctrine of a just war. He believed strongly in such things. At the time I believed him to be wrong. I believed that in wartime everything is permissible to save the lives of troops. By the time I left Viet Nam I agreed with him."

"Thank you, Colonel Stoddard. That will be all." Turning to the JAG colonel, Chalmers said "Your witness."

The JAG colonel attempted to regain ground lost when Chalmers had queried Stoddard.

"Is it your position that soldiers must be careful when they are fighting in built up areas?"

"Yes, Colonel, but Viet Nam seems to be a special case. It has come to represent the sort of war we should not fight. We are to take no casualties of our own while inflicting great casualties on the enemy. That is not possible, yet that is what we are told. In this conflict when we receive fire, we return it. When we are shot at, we must return it. We have operated under very aggressive instructions from our commanders and from MACV. Particularly our commanders. They have told us how to deal with civilians when we encounter them. And anybody who says he isn't aware of what happens, is, in my mind, a liar."

"I am not sure what it is that you have just said, Colonel Stoddard. Do you, or do you not, believe that Major Andrews should be held accountable for what occurred at Yen Song (3)?"

"There is no simple answer I can give you, Colonel. Viet Nam is a land of nightmares. Nothing counts but killing or being killed. The enemy is all around us, but usually we don't know who or where they are. There is a lot of confusion, of listening, of tension and terror."

"Answer my question Colonel."

"He was in a free fire zone . . . ."

"That is not being responsive."

"Sir, I find it difficult to justify what happened at Yen Song (3) either morally or militarily."

"Thank you, Colonel. Thank you. Now. Do you have evidence that Andrews' platoon deliberately massacred villagers or were their deaths accidental?"

"Sir, I can only reaffirm what I have earlier stated. I received all my information from Colonel Jeremiah Barrett, Andrews' battalion commander."

"Yes. Thank you. In your view how should the war be conducted to avoid such slaughter?"

"Sir, an analyst of my acquaintance, Major General Edward Lansdale, insists that almost everything we have done in Viet Nam has been counterproductive. He believes that we have dropped more bombs, fired more rifle rounds, shot more artillery shells than were used in all theaters during World War II by both sides. And this in a small country the size of California. General Lansdale says that the way to avoid involving the civilian population is not to allow H and I fires–harrassing and interdicting artillery shelling, not to designate free fire zones, not to recon by fire. He says that the best way to conduct a counter guerrilla war is with a knife, the worst way is with a bomber; the second best way is with a rifle, the second worst weapon is artillery. And as you know, Sir, we have relied heavily on bombs and artillery in Viet Nam."

After answering a number of other questions to clarify his testimony, Stoddard was dismissed.

Chalmers next said, "I call to the stand Chaplain (Colonel) Paul Eastley. For the record Colonel, state your name and your present position." When the chaplain had done that, Chalmers asked him whether he knew Major Andrews."

"Yes I do."

"How did you come to meet him?"

"Sir, we are both from the same home town–Central City, Nebraska. As a boy I scooped snow from the sidewalks of his family home. I was ten years older than he, but I saw him around town occasionally as we were growing up. Then, to my surprise, I encountered him when he was a new platoon leader in Viet Nam one Sunday when I was conducting services. He marched his platoon to the spot I had chosen for worship. Afterwards we talked. We became good friends."

"How well do you think you knew him?"

"Quite well."

"Do you have an opinion as to whether or not the man you knew in Viet Nam would have been capable of ordering or participating in the slaughter of innocent civilians?"

The presiding judge spoke. "Mr. Andrews, I will comment even if the prosecution does not choose to do so. You are asking for an opinion. Rephrase your question or move on to something else." He glowered at the JAG colonel.

"Yes, Sir. Thank you judge. Chaplain Eastley. Do you know of any evidence that your young friend would have been capable of committing the crimes for which he has here been charged?"

"Mr. Andrews, you are asking a religious man something that is quite difficult. I would not wish to be thought naive. Still, I believe strongly that Satan, the Lightbearer, Beelzebub, the Adversary, the Fallen Angel, the Tempter, or whatever he may be called, is an actual entity eternally pitted against goodness. As such, I also believe that Satan can influence the heart of any man 'continually to do that which is evil in the sight of the Lord.' I believe that, given the right circumstances, any one of us could fall into Satan's hands and do abominable things. Having said that, do I believe that Captain

Andrews committed crimes? He, like all of us, was capable of doing so. Did he? I am convinced he did not."

"Sir? May I add one more thing?"

"Yes, of course, Chaplain."

"There are no military victories in Viet Nam–only tragedies. Our leaders must learn that it is not only hard to die for one's country, it is also hard to kill for it. We should not send boys into war unless we do so with great moral clarity and lasting moral justification."

"Thank you, Chaplain. That will be all."

Chalmers took his seat again, patted his son's arm, and watched as the prosecution approached Chaplain Eastley.

"Chaplain? I see you wear two purple hearts. Were you there at Yen Song (3) on that day? I wonder if you got them for participating in Operation Barrett?"

"Nossir, I did not. And no, I was not there."

"So you have no direct evidence to that about which you have just testified?"

"Not directly, no. But I have many years of experience in the military. During those years I have seen the best and the worst in people . . . ."

"Thank you, Chaplain. That will be all." The colonel walked back to his seat. Looking a little crestfallen, Eastley left the witness stand.

Chalmers spoke. "I would next like to call to the stand Master Sergeant Jan Lech Szigmond." He looked at Doug's anxious face and gave a slow wink.

Looking every inch the soldier, his uniform the best fitting of anyone in the room, immaculate in every respect from white side-walled haircut to brightly polished shoes, Szigmond paced to the front of the room. After taking the oath to speak truthfully "so help me God," he took his seat.

Chalmers stood before him. "You are acquainted with the defendant are you not?"

"Yessir, I am."

"How did you meet?"

"When he arrrived in-country he vas assigned to command ze platoon in Alpha Company where I vas platoon serrgeant. I began to like him because he rreally wanted to learn how to be good officerr. I helped him when I could."

"Did you see him often?"

"Yessir. Every day."

"Did he become a good officer?"

"Yessir. Men follow him willingly. Do always what he say. Zey know he try to carrry out orders and still keep zem alive. Even when zey sick with flu or stomach or dysenterry or cough or feverr, zey try to rremain with unit. Zey not want to be sidelined and zen reassigned to anotherr unit. He became best officerr I have ever worrked with."

"I know it is familiar to those members of the court who have seen duty in Southeast Asia, but please describe combat conditions there, Master Sergeant."

"Yessir. Fight by bits and starts. Sometime go without seeing enemy. Sometime he come at you without warrning. Ambush. Orr an attack on Fire Support Base. Then ve go out on Search and Destroy mission looking for zem. Is strange warr. I know.

"I haf fought with Russian army and killed Hitler's Churrmans. I haf fought with Frrench Forreign Legion and killed Tuaregs in north Africa and Wiet Minh in Frrench Indochina. Now I fight with America and kill Wiet Cong in Wiet Nam. Much experience. Wiet Cong verry good fighterrs. Maybe best.

"Good enough to frrighten many. A few U.S. soldierrs rrun in fear, sometimes leaving wounded frriends behind. Some shit or piss in pants. Some hysterrical and crrying durring VC attack. Some. Not many, but some. Others verry strong, even when VC haf strong attack."

"How would you describe the civilian population in Viet Nam, Master Sergeant?"

"Sometime wery dangerrous. Wiet Cong not wearr uniform. Look like everryone else. Ve werre not only fighting an active warr with Wiet Cong and North Vietnamese soldiers, but ve werre also fighting willagers. Ve haf to watch everryone. Many Wiet Cong

180

sympathizers among people. Don't know why. Maybe because haf relatives in it. Maybe because U.S. and southern government have shelled or bombed zer willages. Maybe because fear rretribution frrom Wiet Cong. Maybe because believe in Wiet Cong mission. Reason not rreally imporrtant. Imporrtant is zat difficult to trrust people.

"Little boy throw hand grrenade into bus loaded with G.I.s. Laundry woman attend Wiet Cong meetings at night. Old woman carrry supplies to Wiet Cong in shoulder baskets. Mourrners at funerral carrry coffin loaded with rrifles. Barber has gun hidden and at night fights with Wiet Cong. People worrk for Wiet Cong. Carry supplies. Hide. Give food. Sometimes haf to fight. Werry confusing. Would say zat in Wiet Nam is no innocent civilian. Werry few citizens unarmed at all times."

"Could you relate this to Yen Song (3)?"

"Yessir. Werry true zer. No innocent civilians. Someone zer planted booby trap along pathway zat kill Lieutenant Crosse. Someone in willage firre rrifle zat kill Catlett and Johnson. Zat not innocent. Knew zem. Good soldiers. Buddies angry. Not even supposed to be people zer. ARVN supposed to ewacuate zem. Everryone zer had helped Wiet Cong. Everryone zer knew location of 48th Local Forrce Battalion. No one warrned Lieutenant Crosse. No one tried to prrotect his soldierrs. Now all dead. All U.S. soldierrs dead. Sad.

"Rule numberr one. USMACV rules allow soldiers to rreconnaisance by fire. Zat means to shoot into area with people to see if anyone shoot back. Didn't do zat. Wiet Cong shoot firrst. MACV says when enemy shoot, is o.k. to use powerr against zem. Even if just one bullet. Artillery. Bombs. Napalm. Machine gun. Whatever we haf. Captain Andrews' platoon yustified in what zey did. Zey were at risk of having more dead men in platoon if zey didn't move on Yen Song (3) shooting. I was once platoon serrgeant of men who werre killed. Good men. Good soldiers. All dead."

"Thank you, Master Sergeant. I have no further questions for this witness."

The JAG colonel strode toward Szigmond.

181

"Master Sergeant, I have listened to you give testimony and have noticed that you must not have been born in the United States."

"Yessir."

"Are you a citizen?"

"Yessir."

"Where were you born?"

"Polshka . . . Poland."

"Were you present at Yen Song (3)?"

"No."

"In fact, had you not already been taken prisoner some months before and, at that time, were being held in a prison camp far away in northern 'Wiet Nam'?"

"Yessir."

"You spoke of having been platoon sergeant for the dead men. In fact, had you not been gone so long that many of those you knew had rotated home and the platoon had been reconstituted more than once to replace dead men, wounded men, and those who had rotated?"

"Yessir"

"Then how can you say that you were still familiar with the personnel of the platoon? I have no other questions of this witness."

Looking cool and unruffled, Szigmond stepped away from the witness stand and took a seat in the audience. As he passed the defense table, holding his right hand close to his chest, he looked at Doug. Their eyes met and Jan gave a thumbs up signal to his former commander that the members of the court could not see.

Chalmers called the post psychiatrist to the stand. In response to questions asked him, the psychiatrist told the court much of what he had weeks earlier explained to Doug. He told of post traumatic stress disorder and how it could affect the lives of those who had fought in Viet Nam, even long after they returned home, and after they had been discharged from the service.

"So soldiers sometimes relive scenes from battle?"

"Yes. In their minds they are back in combat. Commonplace things sometimes cause a veteran to react in wrong ways. The most commonly occurring one is to wake up at night screaming that 'the

182

gooks are coming through the wire.' Or they might dive for cover if a car engine suddenly backfires near them."

"So their minds play tricks on them. Is that correct?"

"Yes. That can happen. And in the case of Major Andrews another factor enters in. I believe he is burdened by many false memories that were created for him during his months of imprisonment. False memories will occur as a result of being given outside information often enough. He was imprisoned under intolerable conditions. He was subjected to barbarous forms of torture. Please understand. All torture is barbarous, but in his case his treatment was particularly inhuman. During those torture sessions, he was repeatedly accused of doing thus and so. Those suggestions were told him so often that he came to believe them. When a person is told such things under physical and mental stress and the pain of torture, false memories can become particularly strong and crowd out of the consciousness the real memories.

"Questioning influences what a person remembers. You might recall reading about the way in which the Chinese communists treated our POWs during the Korean conflict. Their methods came to be known as 'brainwashing.' Some of our men were so stressed out that they rejected most of what they had believed all their lives and adopted new ways of thinking and believing. They had false memories.

"The one in charge, the one who desires to create a false memory in someone must do so by building on a structure of truth. That is, on partial truth. You were there at Yen Song (3) weren't you? You did these things, didn't you? You violated your own ethical and moral standards, didn't you? They make the person agree and agree until false memories are constructed. It is the responsibility of the one who wants to create a false memory always to sound logical and consistent, causing the subject to become illogical and inconsistent."

"You think that something like that may have happened to Major Andrews?

"Yes I do. I examined him as part of the pretrial preparation. He told me much of what he remembered. It was all too pat. Too orderly. Too grisly. I, for one, am convinced that most of what he thinks he "remembers" was forced upon his mind during the months of his imprisonment, and was caused by repeated tortures which began not long after his capture and continued up to the time of his escape."

"Thank you, Sir. You have been a great help."

The JAG colonel approached the witness.

"Is psychiatry an exact science?"

"No it is not."

"As a matter of fact, isn't there a great deal of guessing and assuming involved in it?"

"That is sometimes true. Yes."

"Doesn't its research sometimes focus on the trivial and the unimportant? Why left-handed men are more apt to be color blind? Why children under eight are likely to congregate in certain play groups? And so forth."

"Those things sometimes happen."

"Isn't the research done by psychiatrists sometimes so shoddy it cannot even really be called research? I think, for example, of a doctoral dissertation I once examined. It was two volumes long, each volume about four hundred pages. It was considered a sufficient contribution to knowledge that the author received a Ph.D. for doing it. As I recall, the title was 'The incidence of aggression among football teams as they rode school buses to night games along a selected thirty mile stretch of Highway 66 between 1950 and 1955.' I find such studies at the graduate level to be utterly stupid and insane as well as being totally worthless. Less than worthless. Do you find such 'research' to be important?"

"No, Sir, I do not. But all psychiatric research is not like that and much good has come from . . . ."

"Your conclusions about Major Andrews. Might not another psychiatrist report an utterly different conclusion?"

"That is possible."

"Don't such conclusions depend on the orientation of the specific individual doing the assessment; for example one oriented toward the Rogerian philosophy would conclude differently than someone trained by B.F. Skinner or immersed in the teachings of Carl Jung or Sigmund Freud? Yes or no?"

"Yes. That would possibly be the case.

"Yet they would all be reacting to the same set of facts."

"Yes, Sir. That would be true."

"I have no further questions."

Chalmers Andrews called another witness: Oliver Ensenlaube, a former soldier and member of Doug's platoon who was wounded in an ambush. He limped to the stand, his left leg fused at the knee. He told how he had served under three platoon leaders. Andrews was the best of them.

"Sir, he always had our best interests in mind. We liked him because he led from the front, not from the rear. He was ethical. He did not take shortcuts. I do not recall him ever doing anything bad. And he was effective as a platoon leader."

The JAG lawyer countered.

"Were you present at Yen Song (3)?"

"Nossir."

"Do you believe that people can and do change?"

"Yessir. That can happen."

"I have no further questions."

Chalmers spoke. "I have no other witnesses to call. The Defense rests."

It was time for summations by prosecution and defense counsels. The JAG officer was brief and to the point.

"The Defense has brought witnesses to characterize the defendant as a good, effective, ethical officer. As I listened I thought of a dog whose owner I once knew. The dog was about ten years old. All its life it had been gentle, obedient, and loving. Suddenly one day, for no apparent reason, it went berserk, attacked the little daughter of my friend and killed her. The man still sorrows. The dog was quickly put down.

"I contend that Major Andrews must be put down. He deserves the death penalty. I ask only for him to be sentenced to life. We were told some years ago that the unfortunate inhabitants of Yen Song (3) were killed by the Viet Cong so they could blame the U.S. for the incident. Now we know that was not the case. Lieutenant Colonel Stoddard has testified that there was indeed a massacre at Yen Song (3) caused by U.S. troops, all of whom were later killed by a Viet Cong battalion, save for Major Andrews.

"Colonel Stoddard has told us that his information came from an unimpeachable source–Captain Andrews' battalion commander who was briefly present at the scene and who witnessed the slaughter. Although they were not located and so could not testify here in open court, depositions from three survivors state that the Americans had no effective leadership. It was a unit run amok. The defense has tried to paint a rosier picture. Major Andrews was a nice man. Major Andrews was a good platoon leader. Major Andrews was ethical. Major Andrews was able to discuss the theories of St. Augustine intelligently.

"We know now that he has friends. Yet even his friend, Lieutenant Colonel Donald Stoddard has told us that Major Andrews was burned out, no longer able to function effectively. That he was a man who should have been relieved of duty and reassigned to a noncombat position. That is powerful testimony. We have heard the testimony of others who served under him and they have told us that, in their experience, he was a good officer. Unfortunately neither of them were present at Yen Song (3). We have listened to the cockeyed ideas of a man who has chosen a questionable career for himself as he told us all about PTSD and false memories. We have been patient.

"All of this is beside the point. Members of the Board need only concern themselves with the following questions. Did Major Andrews order the massacre? No. If not, should he have anticipated that his men who had been in combat for weeks and months during which time many were wounded or killed might have reacted badly if they suffered more casualties? Yes. Did Major Andrews act effectively, to prevent his men from doing what they did? No. Did Major Andrews join them in their blood lust? Yes. If any of these items were true, then Major Andrews is guilty of murder and should be judged accordingly. Captain Andrews' troops should not have been fired upon, but they were, and still that did not give them the right to massacre the population of an entire hamlet. Thank you."

Chalmers rose from his seat and walked to stand before the members of the Board. For long moments he stared at each one before turning his gaze toward the next man. Silence–and tension–ruled. Then he spoke.

"Everyone here knows that Major Andrews is my son. As such I would make any sacrifice asked of me for him. But there is more. I am a lawyer with many years of experience. If Major Andrews and I were not related, if he was only a prospective client, I would take this case and argue on his behalf. Why?

"Because as we have here heard the 'evidence' unfolded, it has become clear that the prosecution's foundations are transparent, ephemeral. Founded on a bed of sand. You have all heard of command influence. One wonders if this is an example of such? A person might well ponder who it was in the halls of the mighty who first decided that charges should be levied against Major Andrews and what might have been the basis for his reasoning. Why this desire for Major Andrews to be punished? Why the rush to judgment which caused this court to be convened?

"We have been told that a crime was committed but if one was, we do not know with any assurance who might have been responsible for it. Was it the Viet Cong, as we were first told not long after the event? Or was it American soldiers run amok? Lieutenant Colonel Stoddard has testified that a crime was indeed committed. What is the basis of his belief? He was not present. He gained his knowledge from the meanderings of a man he admits was so drunk he did not even know who it was who listened.

"So we can not be certain that a crime was committed. If one was, it was covered up by General Vernon Moore, then commander of the 11th Brigade of which Alpha Company, Second Battalion was a part. Why? For his own purposes not yet revealed.

"If a crime of the magnitude spoken of here was actually committed, then I suggest that this courtroom is not the proper venue to sit in judgment on it. That 'crime' was committed in a foreign country during time of war many years ago. It should be investigated and any culprits tried, not by our government, but by the government of the Republic of Viet Nam where it supposedly occurred. Has that government tried to do so? Not to my knowledge. One wonders why. Perhaps the initial reason given for the massacre is the correct one, that it was committed by soldiers of the Viet Cong 48th Local Force Battalion in hopes of creating an 'incident' of war crimes which could hopefully then be used to blacken the reputations of our own government and its soldiers.

"The prosecution has called as its only witness Lieutenant Colonel Donald Stoddard. All he could offer was a blatantly hearsay statement from a man who was admittedly dead drunk at the time. His primary point was that Major Andrews had been in combat too long at the time of the assault on Yen Song (3). That is hardly condemnatory. Many over the past few years and others serving there right now have also been in combat 'too long.' Do they deserve court-martial for that reason?

"Indeed, the paucity of evidence submitted by the prosecution reinforces my conviction that this case should have been dismissed out of hand and should never have been heard by a judge and jury. For example:

"The prosecution alleged that there were three survivors and that they had given depositions condemning Major Andrews and the American soldiers. We were told that they could not be found so as to bring them here to testify. Their unfounded statements would have been read into the court record by the prosecution had I not objected. Who were–who are–these three? Do they exist? If so, what happened to them? Why were they able to be found to give depositions but then unable to be located to be brought here? In your deliberations, no weight should be given to this shoddy prosecution effort.

"I called Lieutenant Colonel Stoddard back to the stand and this lone witness for the prosecution spent much time defending my client's character, his ethics, his devotion to duty, his desire to make a real difference. He was joined in those sentiments by Chaplain

(Colonel) Paul Eastley, by Master Sergeant Jan Szigmond and by former Specialist Fourth Class Oliver Ensenlaube.

Sergeant Szigmond further testified at length about conditions faced in Viet Nam by our soldiers. He informed us of training given our soldiers by <u>our</u> government at <u>our</u> training bases. If a single shot is fired at an approaching American force by someone in a hamlet or village, then overwhelming fire power can be brought to bear upon that site. Did that happen here?

"The prosecution has likened my client to a mad dog. I do not think it is proper to speak in that way about one who holds the Medal of Honor. The prosecution has stated that the post psychiatrist has 'cockeyed' ideas. That hardly seems to be the way to refer to a professional man working in a respected area. For all these reasons, I ask that you find my client not guilty."

There was a long silence in the courtroom. Finally the presiding judge cleared his throat and began speaking to the jury, the members of the Board. "You have heard the evidence. It now becomes your responsibility to determine an appropriate judgment in this case. In doing so you may consider extenuating matters. You may take into account the background and character of the accused. You may note his reputation. You may consult his service record which has been sent here for just that purpose. You may consider his traits of behavior, his courage in combat, and in the face of torture by the enemy. You may think about his medals, his fidelity to his commissioning oath. You may take into account the prevailing conditions which existed at the time of the alleged crime. Remember that there is not, and should not be, a statute of limitations for murder, that most grievous of crimes. Yet you can remember that Major Andrews is charged with culpability for things which may have happened years ago. Special circumstances may also be considered. Remember that this man and one other managed to escape from heinous torture and treatment in a prison operated by the military of the Democratic Republic of Viet Nam. All these things and more are now your responsibility.

"You must remember that the best sentence is not one that punishes only. The best sentence is one that reflects the character of our peculiar military society, that holds to our military traditions and goals. It should be a decision which seeks to maintain discipline and which furthers the Army's mission of service to our country. It is one that holds fast to the concepts of duty, honor, country.

"It must be said that, as an officer, Major Andrews may be held to a higher degree than would an enlisted man, but not in such a way that it would impose unrealistic expectations upon the officer corps. Now, if there are no questions, I ask you to retire to begin your deliberations."

The seven men stood and filed from the room. Chalmers reached over and squeezed Doug's arm. "I think we just won our case. Did you listen to him? He was telling them not to convict you! Hot damn!"

Despite Chalmers' enthusiasm, Doug's heart was in his throat. He turned and looked at Nancy, at his mother and sister. Then he and his dad joined the womenfolk. They moved into an adjoining office and sat there. Doug's MP popped his head into the room and asked if they would like coffee. They all did. They continued to talk.

Time dragged. Through Doug's mind ran the words and music of a song from Gilbert and Sullivan's "HMS Pinafore," in which he had performed years earlier in high school. "The hours go on apace." Apace indeed. They could not have passed more slowly. Then the Sergeant at Arms came into the room and announced that the Board members had not yet been able to reach a decision and so the judge was dismissing them for the day. The Board would continue its work. Doug and his lawyer needed only to be back in place by 0800 the next day. They left and sought refuge in Doug's VOQ.

* * * * *

At eight o'clock the next morning, observers had filled the available chairs in the room and some were standing against the rear wall. Doug and Chalmers sat at their desk. So also did the JAG colonel at his. Those at the two tables pointedly ignored the other. The members of the Board filed in and took their places.

The sergeant at arms called out: "All rise."

190

As everyone scrambled to their feet, the presiding judge came into the room and took his seat.

Everyone sat. He then turned to the members of the Board and asked whether or not they had reached a decision.

"We have, Sir."

"Major Andrews, please report to the judge."

Doug rose and walked to within three paces of the judge and saluted him. Then he stood stiffly at attention.

The highest ranking member of the military Board passed a note to the judge who glanced at it and then went back and read it again slowly and carefully. He finally looked at Major Andrews.

"As president of this court, it is my duty to inform you of the decision made unanimously in closed session by the Board members. They have found you guilty of the charges laid against you. This decision was reached after discussion and after a secret ballot, all members concurring. After discussion and then by secret ballot they have unanimously decided upon your sentence. It is as follows:

"1. That you are to be discharged from the Army.

"2. That you will forfeit all pay and allowances due you for past or present service.

"3. That you are to serve not more than three nor less than one year at hard labor while confined at the Disciplinary Barracks, Fort Leavenworth, Kansas.

"4. That you are to be fined one thousand dollars.

"I accept their decision, with but one cavil. You have already been imprisoned in the north of Viet Nam for over two years. Your incarceration there was under much more stringent conditions than those provided for prisoners by the DB. One year there might well be equivalent to two here. In addition you were tortured on a regular basis until you reached the edge of sanity. You have now also been under arrest and detention here at Fort Leavenworth for four months since you were notified of this court-martial. I therefore suspend and set aside that portion of the decision by the Board which called for you to spend more time in prison. You have been confined long enough. I thus reduce this punishment to time served."

The judge held Doug's gaze. Doug saluted him and the salute was returned.

"This decision will be reviewed by higher authority. This court is now closed," the judge announced. He rose from his desk and was surrounded by an onslaught of reporters yammering questions at him. Doug and his father embraced. Nancy quickly moved to them and Doug held her closely as Charlotte and Laura moved up with tears of joy on their cheeks. Joining the group was Chaplain Eastley, Szigmond, Stoddard, Ensenlaube and Dr. Currey who offered their fervent congratulations.

"We're free to go. Let's do it," Chalmers said.

Outside a moment later, Chalmers stopped them all. He reached out and took the hands of both Doug and Nancy.

"You are both being given a second chance. It's a gift from the good Lord. Be grateful. Don't mess it up this time."

* * * * *

EPILOGUE

"Be strong and of good courage, do not fear or be in dread of them; for it is the Lord your God who goes with you; he will not fail you or forsake you." –Deuteronomy XXXI: 6.

That was all a long time ago. Many years have gone by. The Bible speaks of how men and women experience the passage of their days. Check the book of Psalms. "Thou dost sweep men away; they are like a dream, like grass which is renewed in the morning: in the morning it flourishes and is renewed: in the evening it fades and withers."–Psalms XC: 5.

Perhaps closer to the mark is a passage a little later. "My days are like an evening shadow; I wither away like grass."–Psalms CII: 11.

The best description of our lives is in the next chapter of Psalms. "As for man, his days are like grass; he flourishes like a flower of the field; for the wind passes over it, and it is gone, and its place knows it no more."–Psalms CIII:15-16.

All these verses remind us of the impermanence of life. It is here and then it is gone.

Just so, the thirty years following the court-martial of Major Douglas MacArthur Andrews passed more quickly than any of the participants could have imagined. His court-martial convened on 18 January 1971. It closed on 1 February at which time he was freed from further detainment. As he and Nancy left the building it was almost as if they were newly born. Now, finally, they had a life that they could share together. Some of you may be interested in knowing what happened to them in the three decades that followed and to the other people who played such a prominent role in this story.

Douglas MacArthur Andrews. For a time following the court-martial he felt at loose ends, not knowing what to do with his life now that he had been discharged from the Army. One priority was uppermost in his mind. As soon as Nancy's divorce became final, she and Doug married, built a home on the south end of town, and over the next years Doug fathered three children. Earlier, at the time of his marriage, he reasoned that he had always intended at some point to return to his family and to Central City. With his father's encouragement he decided on law school and enrolled at the University of Nebraska. Upon graduation in 1975 he joined his father's law firm in Central City. Later, as his father had done, Doug served as a Nebraska State Senator for three terms. The brutal treatment imposed on him by his captors in North Viet Nam continued to assail him always. At all times his feet hurt with arthritic pain, the vertebrae in his spine tormented him during weather changes, he suffered from headaches due to the kickings given him in prison, and he occasionally commented how it felt like worms were crawling through the bullet wound in his chest left by the *chieu hoi.*

His flashbacks of Yen Song (3) diminished over the years, but not his guilt. He began a program, joined by Nancy, of returning to Viet Nam for a month each year and using that time to offer any desired help—at first to those who had moved to the rebuilt Yen Song (3) and later at various places throughout that country. This activity, he told friends, was one of the major things that gave meaning to his life. He retired from the law firm on his sixtieth birthday. He and Nancy, both members of the local country club can often be seen on the golf links there. They are also prominent members of the Presbyterian Church. They lead a quiet, pleasant life.

Nancy Elaine (West) Dietrich Andrews. The divorce arranged by Chalmers Andrews went through uncontested and quickly. She resigned from the Army Medical Corps, relinquishing her majority rank. She and Doug were united in marriage in the summer of 1971. She became the mother of three children: Brad, Brian, and Brianna. Upon reaching adulthood Brad worked as general manager of the Andrews corporation. Brian attended law school and joined the family firm. Brianna attended law school, married a lawyer, and both worked in Central City at the family firm. For two decades Nancy worked as

194

Head of Nursing at Litzenberg Hospital on the south end of Central City, just off Highway 14, and derived a great deal of satisfaction from being able to continue in her chosen profession. Throughout her marriage she followed Doug on his pilgrimages to Viet Nam and, during that month, volunteered her services at the Tu Du Women's Hospital in Ho Chi Minh City. She now lives quietly in retirement with her husband.

Chalmers Henry Andrews. Vigorous in his mid-fifties at the time of the court-martial, he returned to his practice in Central City. He continued going to the office until his mid-seventies at which time he became "of counsel" for the firm which he had begun and which had been so much a part of his life. As he neared his eightieth birthday his health began a general decline. He was hospitalized several times for a variety of illnesses–removal of a pilonidal cyst, repair of an inguinal hernia, a carotid endarterectomy, removal from his jaw of a mucoepidermoid carcinoma, and a triple bypass. He also developed Type II diabetes. Now in his late eighties and very fragile, his wife jealously guards his time and his health. He is still well enough to go on the occasional cruise with his wife.

Charlotte Elizabeth (Anise) Andrews. All her married life she felt it was her duty and privilege to care for her husband and two children. Then during the Viet Nam conflict she became an active member of 'Get Rid of War' or GROW. She maintained her interest for years. She doted on her five grandchildren and claimed they gave her a new lease on life. She occasionally quoted to Doug and Laura the old saw 'grandchildren are God's gift to parents for not killing their children.' Now in her eighties she is active in church work and volunteers at Hard Memorial Library one afternoon each week. An elderly woman now, she remains a beautiful one.

Laura Alise (Andrews) Bettancourt. Laura graduated from Nebraska Wesleyan University and married Richard Bettancourt, a graduate of the Law School at the University of Nebraska. She took further school work and ultimately became a paralegal. Both she and her husband work at the Andrews family law firm in Central City. They have two children: Barry and Brenda. (It seems that the Andrews prefer names that begin with the letter "B.")

Jonathan Barr Dietrich. He served five years in the Texas State Prison for his crimes against Nancy and disappeared from the lives of all concerned.

Paul Noah Eastley. As his friends had sometimes warned him might happen, in 1976 Chaplain (Colonel) Paul Eastley was called from his position as Commandant of the U.S. Army Chaplain Center and School to become the Deputy Chief of U.S. Army Chaplains with the rank of brigadier general, and spent the next four years at the Pentagon. In 1980 when the current holder of that position retired, he was again promoted, this time to major general, and became the Chief of Chaplains, a statutory four year tour of duty. He retired in 1984. Finally, nearly fifty years of age, he met Teresa Annalise Nappolita, and they married. He is the father of four children. In his retirement, Chaplain Eastley accepted a call to ministry from a small Methodist church in northern California. One wall of his church office is dedicated to reminders of his years in the military and hangs full of pictures, plaques, and shadow boxes filled with ribbons and medals. He has confessed to friends that his civilian life is not nearly as exciting as was his life in the military. He keeps in contact with the Andrews family through Christmas letters. In 1990, on a vacation trip with his wife, Paul stopped in Central City for a grand reunion with the Andrews family.

Vernon Haestack Moore. In 1973 Vernon "Savage" Moore became the subject of an Army investigating committee looking into the incident at Yen Song (3). He had risen in rank from colonel at the time of the Yen Song (3) event to major general. He was found culpable of withholding information from his superiors and of actively heading a massive effort to cover up the occurrence at Yen Song (3). The final report also suggested that, while still commander of the 11th Brigade (Separate), 23rd Division, he may have had some undetermined responsibility in the death of Lieutenant Colonel Jonathan Barrett, commander of the subordinate unit Second Battalion. As a result he was stripped of his decorations and reduced in rank to his permanent grade of colonel. He soon resigned his commission. On the roster of retired officers maintained by the military, his rank of major general was immediately restored for he had held it while on active duty for more than one hundred and eighty days. In retirement he served for some years on the executive boards of several corporations including Enron and Worldcom. He died in 1991.

Donald Benjamin Stoddard. Don stayed in the Army rising rapidly through the ranks. In 1971, at the time of Doug's court-martial, he was an early promoted lieutenant colonel. In 1976 he was selected for promotion to full colonel and in 1980 made his first star. In 1984 he was promoted to major general and in 1986 became a lieutenant general. During his final assignment he worked on the staff at the Office of the Joint Chiefs of Staff. He was destined to be denied the rank of full general, but always told acquaintances that he had done all right for a middle class kid from Pulaski, New York. He retired in 1993.

He married the former Wilhelmine Struthers in 1975 and they had four children. He named his first born, a son, Douglas MacArthur Stoddard, in recognition of his long time friend and of General MacArthur, his lifelong hero. He hoped that he had always been able to uphold the standards MacArthur had held before the cadets at the Military Academy: Duty, Honor, Country.

Jan Lech Szigmond. Following the conclusion of the court-martial Master Sergeant Jan 'Sick Man' Szigmond returned to his job at Fort Lewis and completed his final tour of duty there. Soon after he retired he made a trip of remembrance to Central City to see his longtime friend Doug Andrews. Within two days of his arrival, Doug insisted upon hiring him as foreman for the Andrews family's extensive land holdings covering thousands of acres in Merrick County, farms which raised soy beans, milo, corn and wheat. He would also supervise the commercial grain elevators, the stock pens by the Union Pacific Railroad, and the cattle feeder lots to the east of town operated by the family. For whatever reason, old Josh Andrews, several generations back, had decreed that all the farm buildings would be painted a dull yellow and that custom still held. One of them became his home. Szigmond always maintained that they were the color of stale vomit. To which Doug inevitably responded with the same question. "Jan? How is it that you are so well acquainted with stale vomit?"

Doug believed that if his friend could ramrod the men of a squad, a platoon, a company, then he could certainly control and supervise farm laborers. Szigmond proved him correct. He retained his position until his retirement in 2001 at age seventy. He confided to acquaintances (Doug still believed that he was Szigmond's only friend) that he had come a long way from his beginnings in Grodzisk, Mazowiecki, near Pruszko, southeast of Warszawa . . . then he would correct his speech and slip back into English and identify Warszawa as Warsaw.

In retirement Jan could be found every morning in the donut shop in Central City, drinking coffee and taking an occasional bite of the pastries while regaling those around him with tales of having fought Germans, the Arabic tribesmen of Africa (Tuaregs and Oulad Nails), and the little yellow men of Asia. Afternoons saw the old soldier puttering in his vegetable and flower garden or repairing some item around his cottage. He and Doug saw one another almost every day. Doug raised his children to treasure 'Uncle' Jan, telling them that once upon a time, their 'uncle' had saved daddy's life. Szigmond passed away in his sleep in the winter of 2002 and today occupies a central position in the Andrews family plot in the Central City cemetery. His tombstone bears the flag of Poland with conjoined master sergeant stripes carved into the marble and, below his name, the Latin phrase *Requiescat in Pace*.

Oh yes, there was one other person who played a minor role in this tale.

Cecil Barr Currey. At the end of the court-martial, he returned to his job as a professor of history at Nebraska Wesleyan University but shortly accepted a position at the University of South Florida, Doug's old college. He received several awards there including a state-wide one for his classroom teaching. He also became quite an author, publishing well over twenty books of history, philosophy and religion five or six of which became book club selections and some of them translated into Spanish, Portuguese, French and Chinese. His writings also received attention in Canada and England. He gained an international reputation in his field of military history and came to be listed in *Who's Who in the World*. Upon his retirement the university recognized him as a Professor Emeritus.

Always however the book of which he was most proud was his biography of Douglas MacArthur Andrews, entitled *A Time To Remember*, first published in 1974. Revised and updated, this is that book.

Fall 2003

About The Author

Acclaimed by reviewers here and abroad, award-winning author and well-known university professor of military history Cecil Barr Currey, understands the land, people, and history of Vietnam. Four of his twenty-some nonfiction books have dealt with that nation. His biography of Vietnamese General Vo Nguyen Giap, *Victory at any Cost,* was nominated for a Pulitzer and received the 1997 book award from the prestigious Association of Third World Studies. A selection of the History Book Club, it was simultaneously published in England and was translated into Chinese, French, and Portuguese. His historical writings have brought him international recognition and he is listed in *Who's Who in America* and *Who's Who in the World.* This is his second novel focusing on the American conflict there. The first was *Innocence Dies* (1stBooks Library, 2001). A *Time to Remember* is its sequel, picking up the action from the last pages of the former book and carrying it to a stirring conclusion.

Currey lives with his wife Laura in south Florida.

Printed in the United States
54511LVS00001BB/9